Confirmation, Sacrament of Grace

The theology, practice and law of the Roman Catholic Church and the Church of England

by

James Behrens

Confirmation, Sacrament of Grace

The theology, practice and law of the Roman Catholic Church and the Church of England

James Behrens

Gracewing.

First published 1995
Gracewing
Fowler Wright Books
2 Southern Avenue Leominster
Herfordshire HR6 0QF

Cover design by Rafi Mohamed

Additional typesetting by Action Typesetting Limited, Gloucester

Printed by Progressive Printing, Leigh-on-Sea, Essex SS9 5LQ

ISBN: 0 85244 343 9

Table of Contents

Table of Contents

Table of Contents

Table of Sources and Authorities

BIBLIOGRAPHY

A short guide to the duties of church membership, issued by the Archbishops of
Canterbury and York 1954 -- 81, 82, 99
All God's Children, Church House Publishing 1991 (GS 988) ------------------ 21
Alternative Service Book------------------------------------ 18, 19, 20, 29, 53, 60, 93
Apostolic Constitution *Divinae Consortium Naturae* ----------------------------- 12
Aquinas, St. Thomas: *Summa Theologica* --------------------------------------- 101
Balhoff: Age for Confirmation: Canonical Evidence The Jurist, 45 (1985): 2,
549-587 -- 35, 36
Baptism and Confirmation Today, being the Final Reports of the joint
committees on Baptism, Confirmation, and Holy Communion, as presented
to the Convocations of Canterbury and York in October 1954; London
SPCK 1954 --- 66
Baptism, Eucharist and Ministry, Faith and Order Paper No 111, World
Council of Churches, Geneva 1982 --- 21
Berkhof: Systematic Theology © The Banner of Truth Trust ------------------- 10
Bettenson, Henry: The Early Christian Fathers, Oxford University Press ------- 1
Book of Common Prayer ------------------ 14, 17, 18, 19, 26, 29, 52, 53, 56, 60, 80
Bucer, M: Censura (1551) --- 54
Caparros, Thériault and Thorn: Code of Canon Law Annotated, Wilson &
Lafleur Limitée, Montreal 1993 ----------------------- 29, 31, 34, 35, 36, 51, 85
Chadwick, Henry: The Early Church, revised edition 1993, Pelican Books-- 1, 2
Chevreau, Guy: Catch the Fire, Marshall Pickering, 1994------------------------- 1
Christian Initiation, Birth and Growth in the Christian Society (The Ely
Report), Central Information Office 1971 (GS 30) ---- 4, 7, 15, 21, 52, 66, 67
Church Statistics 1994, Church House Publishing --------------------------------- 5
Coke, Sir Edward: the First Part of the Institutes of the Laws of England, or, a
Commentary upon Littleton--- 71
Communion before Confirmation, Culham College Institute, Abingdon
1993 -- 49, 96
Communion before Confirmation, The report of the General Synod Board of
Education Working Party on Christian Initiation and Participation in the
Eucharist, Chaired by the Bishop of Knaresborough. CIO. 1985 ----------- 36

Table of Sources and Authorities

Table of Sources and Authorities

CANONS OF THE ROMAN CATHOLIC CODE

Canons 879 to 896 are printed in full in the Appendix, page 103

ARTICLES OF THE CHURCH OF ENGLAND

Canon B27 is printed in full in the Appendix, page 107

Table of Sources and Authorities

SCRIPTURAL REFERENCES

Table of Sources and Authorities

RULES OF THE SUPREME COURT

CASES

Preface

My interest in the topic of this book came while studying for the LL.M. degree in Canon Law at Cardiff. In December last year Dr Norman Doe, the director of the course, asked me to lead a seminar on the subject of confirmation for the course weekend in January 1995. The more I researched the subject – and there is far more on the subject than was required just for the seminar – the more interesting I found it, and this work is the result. I am most grateful therefore to Norman for setting alight my interest in confirmation, and for some suggestions as to the areas to research.

I am most grateful to the Revd. Canon Peter Boulton, a fellow student with me in Cardiff, for discussing parts of the liturgy with me, and for drawing to my attention some of the bibliography.

Lastly I wish to express my thanks to my former pupils Justin Higgo and David Drake. Without their assistance I would not have been able to keep up my professional practice and write this book at the same time. Justin has a degree in classics, and so he was also an invaluable help in translating Aquinas.

James Behrens
Lincoln's Inn
July 95

Chapter One

An historical introduction

πληροῦσθε ἐν Πνεύματι[1]

As one theological dictionary states:

> Long before the Spirit was a theme of doctrine, He was a *fact*
> in the experience of the [early Church].[2]

And His presence in the individual was conferred, or confirmed, when that individual was baptised. For in the early church, certainly by the time of Tertullian and Hippolytus of Rome (*c.* 200), the rite of baptism included the laying on of hands, anointing with oil, and prayer for the gift of the Holy Spirit, as well as the baptism with water[3]. During the early centuries of Christianity, it was the bishop alone who presided at the baptismal liturgy.

In the Eastern Church confirmation immediately followed infant baptism and became a part of that rite, whereas in the Western Church, as

---

[1] *pleeroústhe en Pneúmati* , *i.e.* "Be filled with the Spirit"; from Ephesians 5:18.

[2] Eduard Schweizer, 'Pneuma', Theological Dictionary of the New Testament, Eerdmans, Grand Rapids, 1968, vol. VI, p. 396, cited in Guy Chevreau: Catch the Fire, Marshall Pickering, 1994, pages 221-2.

[3] See Cheslyn Jones, The Study of Liturgy, SPCK revised edition 1992, pages 121-2; Henry Chadwick, The Early Church, revised edition 1993, Pelican Books, page 260. In his description of the rite Tertullian writes

> After this when we have come out of the font, we are thoroughly anointed with consecrated oil.

> Thereafter the hand is laid upon us, invoking and inviting the Holy Spirit through the act of blessing

see *De Baptismo*, 7 and 8, cited in Bettenson: The Early Christian Fathers, page 147.

dioceses grew larger, confirmation came to be separated from the baptismal rite, and applied later, when the bishop could get round to it. In the East, the priest took over the bishop's role. In the West, the bishop continued to play a part in the initiation of most Christians through the confirmation rite. The practice of confirmation, as distinct from baptism, by presbyters and deacons developed during the fourth century[4], even though there was some doubt about the legality of this[5].

By the thirteenth century[6], infant confirmation still commanded a fair measure of approval, though it was becoming increasingly uncommon in practice. This was due partly to the rarity of an episcopal visit, partly to the persistent negligence of parents, and partly to a widespread and growing deprecation of confirmation in the minds of church people as a whole[7]. Archbishop Peckham's regulation of 1281, that nobody should be admitted to the sacrament of the Lord's body and blood, save when in danger of death, unless he had been confirmed, or had been reasonably prevented from receiving confirmation, was introduced not so much to prevent persons coming to communion, but to endeavour to secure that everybody in the province eventually received confirmation[8].

The confirmation of infants was still approved in principle, and occasionally took place in England as late as the sixteenth century. Thus Princess Elizabeth, daughter of Henry VIII and later Queen Elizabeth I, who was born on the 7th September 1533, was baptised and confirmed at the same ceremony three days later[9].

---

[4] Henry Chadwick, loc. cit., suggests this was already happening by the year 200.

[5] see Rodríguez *The Minister of Confirmation*, Concilium 8/4 (10/1968), 16-20, and Hans Kung: The Church, Search Press Ltd. 1968, pages 430-1.

[6] For the period from the fourth to the thirteen centuries, see Joseph Martos: Doors to the Sacred, pages 212-222, and J.D.C. Fisher: Christian Initiation: the Reformation Period, pages 159-164.

[7] J.D.C. Fisher: Christian Initiation, Baptism in the Medieval West page 121-2.

[8] J.D.C. Fisher: Christian Initiation, Baptism in the Medieval West page 124.

[9] J.D.C. Fisher: Christian Initiation, Baptism in the Medieval West page 136, referring to H.Holloway, The Confirmation and Communion of Infants (1901), page 44, and S.L. Ollard, Confirmation and the Laying on of Hands

Luther dismissed as a medieval superstition the idea that confirmation gave the Holy Spirit. Writing in 1522, soon after his excommunication, he said

> I allow that confirmation be administered provided that it is known that God has said nothing about it, and knows nothing of it, and that what the bishops allege about it is false. They mock our God saying that it is a sacrament of God, when it is a merely human invention[10].

(1934), page 62. See also Cheslyn Jones: The Study of Liturgy, page 151. A description of what took place is to be found in Carolly Erickson, The First Elizabeth, pages 20 - 21

> The christening could hardly have been more elaborate if the child had been the hoped-for prince. The chief nobles, the leading churchmen and the lord mayor and aldermen stood by as the dowager duchess of Norfolk carried the baby to the church, with Thomas Boleyn behind her bearing the long train of the purple velvet christening mantle. Hangings of cloth of gold and bright tapestries draped the interior of the chapel [the friary church at Greenwich], and soft thick carpets covered the floor. A heavy scent of incense and perfume filled the air, disguising the strong odor of coals burning in a brazier near the font; the brazier provided warmth for the baby while she was undressed behind a curtain, then handed to the bishop of London who immersed the back of her head and her heels in the holy water. Before the purple mantle was put on again *she was anointed on back and breast with the holy oil sacred to royalty* [emphasis added], and given her name.

> Elizabeth's three godparents, the dowager duchess, the old marchioness of Dorset and Thomas Cranmer, archbishop of Canterbury, sponsored her at the font, which was raised to permit the crowds of onlookers to witness the baptism "without pressing too nigh". Then the hundreds of guardsmen standing in attendance lit their torches, and even the tiny taper enclosed in the infant's hand was lit and placed on the altar. The christening gifts were produced, and noblewomen carried them into the palace, to the queen's chamber, where Anne and Henry waited to give their formal blessing to their child.

I am grateful to Mr David Baldwin, sergeant of the Chapel Royal, for drawing this passage to my attention.

[10] J.D.C. Fisher: Christian Initiation: the Reformation Period, page 172.

3

Chapter One

In the Spring of the next year, 1523, Luther said

> Confirmation should not be observed as the bishops desire it.
> Nevertheless we do not find fault if every pastor examines the
> faith of the children to see whether it is good and sincere, lays
> hands on them, and confirms them.[11]

Out of this suggestion grew the Lutheran practice of preparing and
confirming children before they were admitted to the sacrament of the
Lord's table[12].

Calvin described the contemporary Latin rite of confirmation as "one of
the most deadly wiles of Satan"[13]. But he believed that in patristic times
there had been a sort of catechumenate for those who had been baptised as
infants, and that in confirmation they were examined by the bishop, made
a public profession of faith, and were approved by the laying on of
hands[14]. Writing in 1536 he referred to and approved this custom, though
Calvin was mistaken in that no such custom had ever existed[15]. However,
through the influence of Luther, Calvin, and the other reformers,
confirmation ceased to be seen primarily as a sacramental act but rather
an occasion for the candidate to accept responsibility for the promises
which had been made at his baptism[16].

Infant confirmation ceased to be permissible, and came to an end
altogether, in England with the introduction of the Prayer Book of 1549,
in which the rubrics before the Order of Confirmation state that

> none hereafter shall be confirmed but as can say in their
> mother tongue, the articles of the faith, the Lord's Prayer, and
> the ten commandments, and can also answer to such questions
> of this short Catechism, as the Bishop (or such as he shall
> appoint) shall by his discretion appose them in.

---

[11] J.D.C. Fisher: Christian Initiation: the Reformation Period, page 173.

[12] Joseph Martos: Doors to the Sacred, page 223.

[13] see J.D.C. Fisher: Christian Initiation: the Reformation Period, page 254.

[14] Joseph Martos: Doors to the Sacred, page 223.

[15] J.D.C. Fisher: Christian Initiation: the Reformation Period, page 258.

[16] see Christian Initiation, Birth and Growth in the Christian Society (The Ely
Report), paragraphs 4 - 5.

Turning to the twentieth century, the latest statistics available for the Church of England (the provinces of Canterbury and York, but excluding Europe) are for 1993. In that year there were 51,784 confirmations, of whom approximately 82 per cent were over 12 and 45 per cent were over 16[17].

The law and the theology of confirmation are two aspects of the same subject. A proper understanding of the law, and purpose behind the law, involves an understanding of the theology. For, as Garth Moore remarked in his Introduction to English Canon Law,[18]

> the interpretation and administration of the law cannot be satisfactorily conducted without an understanding of what lies behind it. The canonist, therefore, can never be simply a lawyer; he must always be in some measure a theologian, and he will frequently require the assistance of historians.

---

[17] see On the Way (General Synod Report) paragraph 2.4. The Church of England Year Book 1995, Church House Publishing 1995, page 170 uses round numbers, but adds the statistic that of the 52,000 confirmed, 20,000 were males, and 32,000 females. For church statistics generally, see Church Statistics 1994.

[18] Garth Moore: Introduction to English Canon Law, 3rd Ed. page 1.

Chapter Two

The theology of confirmation

*Confirmation is the confirmation **of** the candidates rather than the confirmation **by** them of their faith.*[19]

Confirmation in Scripture

The principal scriptural[20] meaning of the words confirm and confirmation is to establish, ratify, or strengthen a covenant[21]. The words are used in the context of:-

a covenant   Genesis 17:2[22]; Deuteronomy 4:31[23]; Deuteronomy 8:18[24]; 2 Kings 23:3[25]; 1 Chronicles 16:17[26]; Psalm 105:10[27]; Daniel 9:27[28]

---

[19] Christian Initiation, Birth and Growth in the Christian Society (The Ely Report), paragraph 8.

[20] All scriptural quotations are from the New International Version of the Bible.

[21] Nelson's Illustrated Bible Dictionary © 1986, Thomas Nelson Publishers, *sub nom.* Confirm.

[22] 2 I will confirm my covenant between me and you and will greatly increase your numbers."

[23] 31 For the LORD your God is a merciful God; he will not abandon or destroy you or forget the covenant with your forefathers, which he confirmed to them by oath.

[24] 18 But remember the LORD your God, for it is he who gives you the ability to produce wealth, and so confirms his covenant, which he swore to your forefathers, as it is today.

[25] 3 The king stood by the pillar and renewed the covenant in the presence of the LORD- to follow the LORD and keep his commands, regulations and decrees with all his heart and all his soul, thus confirming the words of the covenant written in this book. Then all the people pledged themselves to the covenant.

[26] 17 He confirmed it to Jacob as a decree, to Israel as an everlasting covenant:

[27] 10 He confirmed it to Jacob as a decree, to Israel as an everlasting covenant:

Chapter Two

a letter	Esther 9:29[29]
a people's identity	Deuteronomy 29:13[30]
a person's words	1 Kings 1:14[31]; Hebrews 6:16[32]
a promise	2 Chronicles 1:9[33]; Romans 15:8[34]; Hebrews 6:16-17[35]
a vow or pledge	Numbers 30:13, 14[36]
an oath	Genesis 26:3[37]; Psalm 119:106[38]
regulations	Esther 9:32[39]

---

[28] 27 He will confirm a covenant with many for one 'seven'. In the middle of the 'seven' he will put an end to sacrifice and offering. And on a wing [of the temple] he will set up an abomination that causes desolation, until the end that is decreed is poured out on him."

[29] 29 So Queen Esther, daughter of Abihail, along with Mordecai the Jew, wrote with full authority to confirm this second letter concerning Purim.

[30] 13 to confirm you this day as his people, that he may be your God as he promised you and as he swore to your fathers, Abraham, Isaac and Jacob.

[31] 14 While you are still there talking to the king, I will come in and confirm what you have said."

[32] 16 Men swear by someone greater than themselves, and the oath confirms what is said and puts an end to all argument.

[33] 9 Now, LORD God, let your promise to my father David be confirmed, for you have made me king over a people who are as numerous as the dust of the earth.

[34] 8 For I tell you that Christ has become a servant of the Jews on behalf of God's truth, to confirm the promises made to the patriarchs

[35] 16 Men swear by someone greater than themselves, and the oath confirms what is said and puts an end to all argument.
17 Because God wanted to make the unchanging nature of his purpose very clear to the heirs of what was promised, he confirmed it with an oath.

[36] 13 Her husband may confirm or nullify any vow she makes or any sworn pledge to deny herself.
14 But if her husband says nothing to her about it from day to day, then he confirms all her vows or the pledges binding on her. He confirms them by saying nothing to her when he hears about them.

[37] 3 Stay in this land for a while, and I will be with you and will bless you. For to you and your descendants I will give all these lands and will confirm the oath I swore to your father Abraham.

[38] 106. I have taken an oath and confirmed it, that I will follow your righteous laws.

salvation	Hebrews 2:3[40]
testimony	1 Corinthians 1:6[41]
the choice of a person as king	1 Samuel 11:15[42]
the gospel	Philippians 1:7[43]; Acts 14:3[44]
the truth	Romans 9:1[45]
the word of the Lord	Mark 16:20[46]
wisdom	Job 28:27[47]
writing	Acts 15:27[48]

From these texts we see that the main use of the word is to establish, ratify, or strengthen a covenant obligation entered into between God and His chosen people. The covenant relationship is an important concept in

---

[39] 32 Esther's decree confirmed these regulations about Purim, and it was written down in the records.

[40] 3 how shall we escape if we ignore such a great salvation? This salvation, which was first announced by the Lord, was confirmed to us by those who heard him.

[41] 6 because our testimony about Christ was confirmed in you.

[42] 15 So all the people went to Gilgal and confirmed Saul as king in the presence of the LORD. There they sacrificed fellowship offerings before the LORD, and Saul and all the Israelites held a great celebration.

[43] 7. It is right for me to feel this way about all of you, since I have you in my heart; for whether I am in chains or defending and confirming the gospel, all of you share in God's grace with me.

[44] 3 So Paul and Barnabas spent considerable time there, speaking boldly for the Lord, who confirmed the message of his grace by enabling them to do miraculous signs and wonders.

[45] 1. I speak the truth in Christ- I am not lying, my conscience confirms it in the Holy Spirit-

[46] 20 Then the disciples went out and preached everywhere, and the Lord worked with them and confirmed his word by the signs that accompanied it.

[47] 27 then he looked at wisdom and appraised it; he confirmed it and tested it.

[48] 27 Therefore we are sending Judas and Silas to confirm by word of mouth what we are writing.

understanding the theology of baptism[49]. The use of the word confirmation in the Christian church is a reminder of the use of the word in scripture, and of the theology of baptism. The word indicates that God is ratifying or strengthening the covenant relationship between Himself and the Christian which came into existence when the Christian first believed or was baptised[50]. By the Middle Ages (*c.* 900) the Church interpreted the Latin *confirmare* as meaning *to strengthen*[51].

The scriptural references most closely associated[52] with the practice of confirmation as a church service or sacrament are Acts 8:14-17[53], Acts 19:1-7[54], and Hebrews 6:1-3[55], the passage from Acts 19 being the *locus*

---

[49] See Reardon: Christian Initiation - A policy for the Church of England, pages 19, 57–64, Hammond: In Understanding Be Men, pages 171-172, Lampe: The Seal of the Spirit *passim*

[50] By the thirteenth century the sense of strength to bear witness and resist temptation became widespread. With the 1662 Book of Common Prayer the individual acceptance of the promises made at baptism became established. See On the Way, section 4.48. The theological controversy whether or not baptism is (a) *necessary* or (b) *sufficient* for salvation is beyond the scope of this study. In the Catholic Church baptism is "necessary for salvation in fact or at least in intention": Canon 849 of the Catholic Code. The Church of England does not hold this position: see Article VI, Article XI, Article XVIII and Article XXVII of the Church of the England. Both churches of course approve the practice of infant baptism: see Canon 867 and Canon 868 of the Catholic Code, and Article XXVII of the Church of England.

[51] see J.D.C. Fisher: Christian Initiation: Baptism in the Medieval West pages 141-148, and Cheslyn Jones: The Study of Liturgy, pages 148-150.

[52] see Berkhof: Systematic Theology © The Banner of Truth Trust, page 620.

[53] 14. When the apostles in Jerusalem heard that Samaria had accepted the word of God, they sent Peter and John to them.
15 When they arrived, they prayed for them that they might receive the Holy Spirit,
16 because the Holy Spirit had not yet come upon any of them; they had simply been baptised into the name of the Lord Jesus.
17 Then Peter and John placed their hands on them, and they received the Holy Spirit.

[54] 1. While Apollos was at Corinth, Paul took the road through the interior and arrived at Ephesus. There he found some disciples

classicus. From these verses one sees the following elements: the laying on of hands, the receiving of the Holy Spirit, that this takes place at the same time as or after baptism, is part of Christian initiation, and in some way strengthens the new Christian in his walk with the Lord.

The Roman Catholic Church

The Catholic church holds that confirmation is a sacrament. Sacraments are described by Canon 840 as follows:

> The sacraments of the New Testament were instituted by Christ the Lord and entrusted to the Church. As actions of Christ and of the Church, they are signs and means by which faith is expressed and strengthened, worship is offered to God and our sanctification is brought about. Thus they contribute in the most effective manner to establishing, strengthening and manifesting ecclesiastical communion. Accordingly, in the celebration of the sacraments both the sacred ministers and the other members of Christ's faithful must show the greatest reverence and due care.

---

2 and asked them, "Did you receive the Holy Spirit when you believed?" They answered, "No, we have not even heard that there is a Holy Spirit."
3 So Paul asked, "Then what baptism did you receive?" "John's baptism," they replied.
4 Paul said, "John's baptism was a baptism of repentance. He told the people to believe in the one coming after him, that is, in Jesus."
5 On hearing this, they were baptised into the name of the Lord Jesus.
6 When Paul placed his hands on them, the Holy Spirit came on them, and they spoke in tongues and prophesied.
7 There were about twelve men in all.
[55] 1. Therefore let us leave the elementary teachings about Christ and go on to maturity, not laying again the foundation of repentance from acts that lead to death, and of faith in God,
2 instruction about baptisms, the laying on of hands, the resurrection of the dead, and eternal judgment.
3 And God permitting, we will do so.

Canon 842 § 2 states

> The sacraments of baptism, confirmation and the blessed
> Eucharist so complement one another that all three are
> required for full Christian initiation

Canon 879 describes[56] the sacrament of confirmation.

> The sacrament of confirmation confers a character. By it the
> baptised continue their path of Christian initiation. They are
> enriched with the gift of the Holy Spirit, and are more closely
> linked to the Church. They are made strong and more firmly
> obliged by word and deed to witness to Christ and to spread
> and defend the faith.

Canon 880 describes how confirmation is effected.

> the sacrament of confirmation is conferred by anointing with
> chrism on the forehead, which is done by the laying on of the
> hand, and by the words prescribed in the approved liturgical
> books.
> The chrism to be used in the sacrament of confirmation must
> have been consecrated by a Bishop, even when the sacrament is
> administered by a priest.

Before the Apostolic Constitution *Divinae Consortium Naturae* of 15
August 1971, which promulgated the new rite of confirmation, there were
several different theories held by Catholic theologians about the effect of
the sacrament. The main views were: (1) the sacrament was the last stage
in the process by which a person became a member of the Church
(baptism and first communion being the other main stages); (2) it
endowed the candidate with the Holy Spirit to give him strength to be
Christ's witness; (3) it endowed him with the Holy Spirit to strengthen
him for all the difficulties of Christian living; (4) it was a sacrament of
commitment by which a baptised Christian reaffirmed in a more mature
way his faith in Christ and his entry into the Church which began at
baptism. The Holy Father in this Apostolic Constitution used only the
first and second ways of describing the effects of confirmation.

---

[56] or, perhaps, defines

12

Thus the Rite of Confirmation describes the effect of Confirmation as follows:[57]

> In the sacrament of Confirmation those who have been reborn in Baptism receive the Holy Spirit, the priceless Gift, by which they are endowed with special strength, and signed with the character of a sacrament, are more perfectly united to the Church, and obliged, as true witnesses of Christ, in word and deed more strongly to spread and defend the faith.

According to Catholic theology the Apostles gave the Holy Spirit to those who had been baptised by laying their hands on them. The bishop performs the same sign when he touches the candidate's forehead with chrism. This action, together with the words, "[Name], be sealed with the Gift of the Holy Spirit", is the essential part of the ceremony.

Chrism is oil mixed with a perfume. The oil signifies strength. The perfume stands for the attractiveness of a Christian life, the life of Christ himself within us: see 2 Corinthians 2:15[58] The witness of Christ needs both the strength and the attractiveness.[59]

[60]The sign of the cross on the forehead is a seal. When you fix a seal on a document, you prove that it is genuine; Christ's seal, the sign of His cross, proves that the candidate is one of his followers. Of course the mark of the oil soon gets rubbed away from the forehead; but Christ's seal lasts for ever. Once we have been confirmed, we are his followers and his witnesses for ever; even if we should prove unfaithful to him, this seal (or character) remains, not on our foreheads but in our hearts. The Holy Spirit is our Lord's gift to us, just as God the Father gave the Holy Spirit to our Lord when he was baptised. The gift God gives us

---

[57] Rite of Confirmation (including an introduction and commentary) © 1972 and 1975 St Paul Publications

[58] 15 For we are to God the aroma of Christ among those who are being saved and those who are perishing.

[59] Rite of Confirmation (including an introduction and commentary) © 1972 and 1975 St Paul Publications

[60] This paragraph is also taken from the Rite of Confirmation (including an introduction and commentary) © 1972 and 1975 St Paul Publications

strengthens us to be his witness, just as the Holy Spirit strengthened our Lord to be God the Father's witness: John 20: 21-22[61].

The Church of England

In the Church of England, Article XXV stresses that confirmation, together with the four other commonly called Sacraments, namely Penance, Orders, Matrimony and extreme Unction

> are not to be counted for Sacraments of the Gospel, being such as have grown partly of the corrupt following of the Apostles, partly are states of life allowed in the Scriptures; but yet have not like nature of Sacraments with Baptism, and the Lord's Supper, for that they have not any visible sign or ceremony ordained of God

Similarly, in the catechism the candidate is asked how many sacraments Christ ordained in his church. The answer to be given is, Two only, as generally necessary to salvation, that is to say, Baptism, and the Supper of the Lord[62].

A definition saying merely what something is not is hardly a good definition. In contrast to the Roman Catholic law, the Church of England does not define the effect of or significance of confirmation. The simplest description of confirmation is that of the rubric to the order of confirmation in the Book of Common Prayer

> The Order of Confirmation, or laying hands upon those that are baptised and come to years of discretion.

---

[61] 21 Again Jesus said, "Peace be with you! As the Father has sent me, I am sending you."

22 And with that he breathed on them and said, "Receive the Holy Spirit."

[62] Strictly, Article XXV does not say that confirmation is not a sacrament, merely that it is not a sacrament of the gospel. Evangelical theology teaches that it is not a sacrament at all.

The description in Halsbury's Laws of England 4th Ed., Vol. 14 paragraph 999 adds to this simple formula a statement that confirmation is carried out by the bishop, and after instruction in the Christian faith[63].

> Confirmation is the laying on of hands by the bishop upon persons who are baptised and instructed in the Christian faith and are come to years of discretion.

The precise theological significance of confirmation is a matter of some dispute within the Church of England. Garth Moore's comment "The Church of England, whilst insisting on its importance, is singularly silent as to its meaning"[64] is inaccurate. Much has been written on the subject. What can be said is that theologians are not united in their understanding of the rite[65].

> There are broadly three schools of thought in the Church of England on the relation of baptism and confirmation:
> i.   Baptism is the sole and complete rite of Initiation; there is no need for any other rite before admission to Communion, except possibly reaffirmation of vows.
> ii. Confirmation, with its baptismal reaffirmation, marks and empowers the Christian at the point of entry into adult life.
> iii. The sacramental aspect of confirmation, *i.e.* prayer for the gift of the Spirit with laying on of hands, completes (along

---

[63] relying on Canon B27, paragraphs 1 and 3.

[64] Moore: Introduction to English Canon Law 3rd Ed. page 64. Hill's Ecclesiastical Law at page 298 correctly states

> There is no clear theological justification for confirmation as a rite separate from baptism

but then copies Garth Moore's mistake, saying

> The Church of England stresses its importance but says little as to its meaning.

[65] *e.g.* Baptism and Confirmation Today. Three members of the committee could not agree with the majority, and wrote their own minority report. Christian Initiation, Birth and Growth in the Christian Society (The Ely Report) at paragraph 3 described confirmation as "a rite in search of a convincing theological justification for its existence".

> with Communion) the rite of initiation, being understood
> as signifying the gift of the Spirit in initiation.[66]

The key moment in the confirmation service is the moment when the
bishop lays his hand on the candidate's head and prays

> Confirm, O Lord, your servant [Name] with your Holy Spirit.[67]

Scripture tells us much about the Holy Spirit. The Holy Spirit is the
power by which Christians are brought to faith and helped to understand
their walk with God[68]. He brings a person to new birth: John 3:6[69], John
6:63[70]. The Holy Spirit is the Paraclete[71], or Helper, whom Jesus
promised to the disciples after His ascension. The Trinity of the Father,
Son, and Holy Spirit together minister to believers: John 14:16, 17, 26[72].
It is through the Holy Spirit that the Father and the Son abide with the
disciples: John 15:26[73].

But

> The precise relation between the gift bestowed in Baptism and
> the gift bestowed in Confirmation cannot be defined. Attempts
> to explain it are as old as Tertullian and Augustine. A clear-

---

[66] see Ecumenical Relations: Canons B43 and B44: Code of Practice, page 28.

[67] The Alternative Service Book form

[68] Nelson's Bible Dictionary, *sub nom.* Holy Spirit

[69] 6 Flesh gives birth to flesh, but the Spirit gives birth to spirit.

[70] 63 The Spirit gives life; the flesh counts for nothing. The words I have
spoken to you are spirit and they are life.

[71] *i.e.* advocate.

[72] 16 And I will ask the Father, and he will give you another Counsellor to be
with you for ever-
17 the Spirit of truth. The world cannot accept him, because it neither sees
him nor knows him. But you know him, for he lives with you and will be in
you.
26 But the Counsellor, the Holy Spirit, whom the Father will send in my
name, will teach you all things and will remind you of everything I have said
to you.

[73] 26 But the Counsellor, the Holy Spirit, whom the Father will send in my
name, will teach you all things and will remind you of everything I have said
to you.

cut answer is impossible, since originally the two were closely conjoined.[74]

Put simply, but not irreverently, one issue is whether confirmation is a conferral or a catalyst, a bestowal or a boosting, of the Holy Spirit's presence[75]. Another is whether the laying on of hands and prayer for the Holy Spirit is sacramental, or precatory, or merely declaratory[76].

If one examines the different liturgies for the confirmation service, one sees these different theological emphases. Starting with the Book of Common Prayer, the Preface begins with the words "To the end that Confirmation may be ministered to the more edifying of such as shall receive it" The service is therefore *edifying* and it is *ministered*. The bishop prays "Strengthen them[77], we beseech thee, O Lord, with the Holy Ghost the Comforter" Does the strengthening happen *as a result of* the bishop laying his hands, or is the laying of hands merely the *occasion* for

---

[74] Doctrine in the Church of England, page 188.

[75] For the view that the Holy Spirit is conferred at confirmation and not at baptism, see Mason, A.J: The Relation of Confirmation to Baptism 1890, 1891, and Dix, G: The Theology of confirmation in Relation to Baptism, 1946. For the more orthodox view, *i.e.* that the Holy Spirit's presence has been in the Christian before confirmation, see Lampe, G.W.H.: The Seal of the Spirit, Longmans 1951

[76] For the declaratory view, see John Stott: Your Confirmation, Hodder and Stoughton 1958 pages 11-13. He describes the confirmation service as an opportunity for the candidate to declare himself a Christian, and to be declared by God a Christian by the increase of the Holy Spirit's presence in the candidate's life. Interestingly, the declaration by the candidate corresponds to the fourth of the Catholic views of confirmation, prior to the 1971 rite, see page 12 *supra*. See further Baptism and Confirmation Today at page 44: "The primary thing in Confirmation is what *God does* for us – imparting his divine strength and further gifts of his Spirit. Yet *our part* is also significant; for we personally dedicate ourselves to our vocation as Christ's soldiers and servants in a public act of witness".

[77] that is, the candidates for confirmation

17

the bishop to pray the prayer? The prayer[78] when the bishop lays his hands on the candidate

> Defend, O Lord, this thy Child [or *this thy servant*] with thy heavenly grace, that *he* may continue thine for ever; and daily increase in thy holy Spirit more and more, until *he* come unto thy everlasting kingdom.

is equivocal as to any sacramental quality. Construed strictly it appears to be merely a prayer for the future, devoid of any sacramental quality. But one might ask whether most candidates see it only in that light.

The sacramental element is even more explicit in the Preface to the Deposited Book of 1928

> The Scripture [*i.e.* Acts 8:14-17[79]] here teaches us that a special gift of the Holy Spirit is bestowed through laying on of hands with prayer. And forasmuch as this gift comes from God alone, let us who are here present pray to Almighty God, that he will strengthen with his Holy Spirit in Confirmation those who in Baptism were made his children.

In the service according to the Alternative Service Book[80], the bishop stretches out his hands towards the candidates and says

> Almighty and ever-living God, you have given your *servants* new birth in baptism by water and the Spirit, and have forgiven

---

[78] Book of Common Prayer form

[79] 14. When the apostles in Jerusalem heard that Samaria had accepted the word of God, they sent Peter and John to them.

15 When they arrived, they prayed for them that they might receive the Holy Spirit,

16 because the Holy Spirit had not yet come upon any of them; they had simply been baptised into the name of the Lord Jesus.

17 Then Peter and John placed their hands on them, and they received the Holy Spirit.

[80] There are in fact three forms of service set out in the Alternative Service Book, an order for service for the baptism and confirmation of adults, an order of service for the baptism of families and confirmation of adults, and an order of service for the confirmation of those already baptised.

> *them* all *their* sins. Let your Holy Spirit rest upon *them*: the
> Spirit of wisdom and understanding; the Spirit of counsel and
> inward strength; the Spirit of knowledge and true godliness;
> And let *their* delight be in the fear of the Lord.

The words "Let your Holy Spirit" could be interpreted as merely a prayer,
not a sacramental act. The words "rest upon" in the Alternative Service
Book was carefully chosen from Isaiah 11:2 (RSV)[81] to reflect the
differing views in the Church of England on whether the Holy Spirit was
conferred by confirmation.[82] Contrast the words "strengthen them" in the
Book of Common Prayer service which perhaps suggests that the
candidates do not already have the Holy Sprit, and the Preface to the
Deposited Book of 1928, which certainly suggests this.

The words (in the Alternative Service Book) used by the bishop when he
lays his hand on the head of each candidate

> Confirm, O Lord, your servant [Name] with your Holy Spirit.

are not in the subjunctive tense. Does the bishop have the right to use the
imperative tense to the Almighty? It appears very much a sacramental
form of words, similar to the Roman Catholic "Be sealed with the Gift of
the Holy Spirit", and not merely precatory.

The prayer in the Alternative Service Book for those who have just been
confirmed is as follows:

> Heavenly Father, we pray for your *servants* upon whom we
> have now laid our hands, after the example of the apostles, to
> assure *them* by this sign of your favour towards *them*. May
> your fatherly hand ever be over *them*, your Holy Spirit ever be
> with *them*. Strengthen *them* continually with the body and
> blood of your Son, and so lead *them* in the knowledge and
> obedience of your word, that in the end *they* may obtain
> everlasting life; through Jesus Christ our Lord.

---

[81] And the Spirit of the LORD shall rest upon him, the spirit of wisdom and
understanding, the spirit of counsel and might, the spirit of knowledge and
the fear of the LORD. (RSV)

[82] see Cheslyn Jones: The Study of Liturgy, page 173

This is precatory in tone ("May your fatherly hand ...").

The whole confirmation process, including both the preparatory teaching which precedes the service and the ceremony itself, contributes to the strengthening of the young Christian. And the prayers at the service are that the Holy Spirit may continue to do this in the future. Confirmation is seen as a complement to baptism, and together with the first communion make up the full Christian initiation[83].

It should be noted that in both the Church of England and in the Roman Catholic Church, confirmation is not the only occasion on which the vows made at baptism may be repeated. In addition to the separate provision in Holy Week and Easter the Alternative Service Book has an order of service[84] entitled "the Renewal of Baptismal Vows on Various Occasions". The service may be used at Easter, at New Year, on other suitable occasions, and in conjunction with a baptism, confirmation and holy communion. In the service

> we renew the promises made at our baptism, affirming our allegiance to Christ, and our rejection of all that is evil.

and the responses are said by all the congregation. The Roman Catholic Church has a similar rite as part of the Easter Vigil celebrations: see the Rite of Christian Initiation of Adults[85]Rite of Christian Initiation of Adults, approved for use in the dioceses of the USA, Study Edition,

---

[83] Two points are noteworthy. First, page 211 of the Alternative Service Book groups the baptism services and confirmation services under the heading "Initiation Services". Second, the Alternative Service Book's principal service of initiation for adults is a service of baptism, confirmation and holy communion. The concept of what constitutes adult Christian initiation is therefore identical for the Roman Catholic Church and the Church of England. Compare Canon 842 § 2 of the Roman Catholic Code, see page 12 *supra*.

[84] pages 275-278, also Lent, Holy Week and Easter pages.

[85] I have used throughout the American study edition of the Rite of Christian Initiation of Adults, published by Liturgy Training Publications, Chicago 1988. This contains some additional rites which are commonly used in Britain, see On the Way paragraph 3.14.

Liturgy Training Publications, Chicago 1988 paragraphs 237-240, and paragraph 580, or in the Roman Missal, "Easter Vigil" (no. 46).

Despite the lack of theological clarity in the Church of England as to the meaning of confirmation[86], the Church of England has a developed practice concerning confirmation, and confirmation has both legal requirements and legal consequences. These will be considered below.

---

[86] See further Doctrine in the Church of England (1938), pages 186-9; Christian Initiation, Birth and Growth in the Christian Society (The Ely Report), chapters 1 and 4; Communion before Confirmation; Christian Initiation - a Policy for the Church of England; All God's Children; Baptism, Eucharist and Ministry.

Chapter Three

The legal effects of confirmation

The Roman Catholic Church

Confirmation is not just a sacrament and a means of grace: it has legal consequences in the Roman Catholic Church. Proof of confirmation is required for admission to a religious institute[87] or to a seminary[88]. Although not strictly necessary for the validity of a sacramental marriage,

> If they can do so without serious inconvenience, Catholics who have not yet received the sacrament of confirmation are to receive it before being admitted to marriage.[89]

Nor is it necessary to be confirmed in order to receive the Eucharist. Baptism is necessary; but confirmation is not. Canon 912 provides

> Any baptised person who is not prohibited by law can and must be admitted to Holy Communion.

This is qualified in the case of children by Canon 913. Two conditions are required for the communion of children; sufficient use of reason and adequate preparation[90]. Children are presumed to have the use of reason at the age of seven years[91], and so this is the age at which they are normally admitted to communion. Confirmation is not a prerequisite for communion, nor *vice-versa*. As for adequate preparation, significantly

---

[87] Canon 645. A dispensation from confirmation could be granted under Canons 85-93 for a just and reasonable cause (see Canon 90). Coriden, Green and Heintschel: The Code of Canon Law, A text and commentary, do not discuss the possibility.

[88] Canon 241. As to dispensations, see Canons 85-93.

[89] Canon 1065

[90] An exception is made in the case of children in danger of death: Canon 913 § 2.

[91] Canon 97 § 2

less is required for communion than for confirmation[92]. Many children take communion for years before they are confirmed[93].

As might be expected, confirmation is a prerequisite for orders[94]. Sponsors for the baptism or confirmation of another must themselves be confirmed[95]. It is also strictly a legal duty for the faithful to receive the sacrament at the appropriate time[96], though this is primarily a duty for the whole Christian community[97], and in the case of children and young persons, the responsibility of their parents and pastors[98].

Various offices in the church are open to lay persons. They can be judges[99], defenders of the bond and promoters of justice[100], advocates[101], assessors[102], auditors[103] and chancellors[104]; they may serve on diocesan finance committees[105], diocesan pastoral councils[106] and the parish

---

[92] see Coriden, Green and Heintschel: The Code of Canon Law, A text and commentary, page 652, referring to "formative experiences in faith such as are promoted by active participation in the Eucharist even before the children receive their first Holy Communion. The liturgy itself has formative value, especially when it is adapted to the children's level as suggested by the principles contained in the *Directory on Children's Masses*. The use of the approved Eucharistic prayers for children can also encourage greater participation in and a fuller understanding of the 'mystery of Christ' referred to in the canon."

[93] The age at which children are confirmed is discussed in Chapter 5.

[94] Canon 1033

[95] Canon 874, § 3, and Canon 893 § 1.

[96] Canon 890

[97] see Quinlan: Parental Rights and Admission of Children to the Sacraments of Initiation, *Studia Canonica*, 25 (1991), pp. 385-401

[98] Canon 890; also Coriden, Green and Heintschel: The Code of Canon Law, A text and commentary page 638

[99] Canon 1421

[100] Canon 1435

[101] Canon 1483

[102] Canon 1424

[103] Canon 1428

[104] Canon 482

[105] Canon 482

council[107]. Nowhere in the Code is it expressly stated that all such persons must be confirmed, but it is arguable that this is the position.

Support for this proposition is to be found in Canon 149, which says

> In order to be promoted to an ecclesiastical office, a person must be in the communion of the Church as well as suitable, namely endowed with those qualities which are required for the office in question by universal or particular law or by the law of the foundation[108]

Caparros, Thériault and Thorn in their commentary on this Canon say[109]

> Canon 149 does not, however, explain what is meant by "communion with the church", although it seems obvious that the expression goes beyond the purely negative fact of not being an excommunicate. The requirement seems to be a positive one which can be demonstrated by the candidate's communion with the lawful pastors, acceptance of their teaching, and participation in the true means of vivifying and uniting the Church community. The profession of faith and oath of fidelity are also required for some offices (cf. Canon 833)

It is thus at least arguable that persons who have not been confirmed would not satisfy the requirements of Canon 149; but this does appear to be a *lacuna*.

---

[106] Canon 512

[107] Canon 536

[108] Canon 149

[109] Caparros, Thériault and Thorn: Code of Canon Law Annotated, page 157

Chapter Three

The Church of England

Subject to certain exceptions holy communion is available only to
confirmed members of the Church of England or persons who are ready
and desirous to be confirmed[110]. Canon B15A provides

> 1. There shall be admitted to the Holy Communion
> (a) members of the Church of England who have been
> confirmed in accordance with the rites of that Church or are
> ready and desirous to be so confirmed or who have been
> otherwise episcopally confirmed with unction or with the
> laying on of hands except as provided by the next following
> Canon.
> (b) baptised persons who are communicant members of other
> Churches which subscribe to the doctrine of the Holy Trinity,
> and who are in good standing in their own Church.
> (c) any other baptised persons authorised to be admitted under
> regulations of the General Synod; and
> (d) any baptised person in immediate danger of death.

In the early centuries of the Church of England, confirmation had not been
seen as a necessary precondition for admission to Holy Communion.
Archbishop Peckham's regulation issued at the Council of Lambeth in
1281 barring admission to those not confirmed or not reasonably
prevented from receiving Confirmation was

> but a matter of discipline directed against the 'damnable
> negligence' of parents content only to have their children
> baptised.[111]

The inclusion of the phase "ready and desirous to be confirmed" can be
traced back to the rubric at the conclusion of the Order of Confirmation in
the Book of Common Prayer. The phrase was a concession by the
bishops to the Puritan divines who at the Savoy conference of 1661 had
stated that "confirmation may not be made so necessary to the Holy
Communion, as that none should be admitted to it unless they be

---

[110] Canon B15A par. 1 and the Rubric at the end of the Order for Confirmation
in the Book of Common Prayer.
[111] Communion before Confirmation, page 10

26

confirmed"[112]. The reason was partly pragmatic. Many persons had not been confirmed during the period of the commonwealth. Generally it may be assumed that persons are only likely to be "ready and desirous" for a relatively short time, *i.e.* until the bishop is next available. However in the case of the overseas diocese and the Channel Islands, there may be a considerable delay before a bishop is available to confirm candidates[113].

Candidates for ordination as deacons or priests must be confirmed[114]. Sponsors and godparents for persons being baptised must be confirmed[115], as must women deacons[116], deaconesses[117] lay readers[118], and lay workers[119].

The positions of chancellor, judges of the arches court of Canterbury and of the chancery court of York, and registrars are governed by Canon G2, Canon G3 and Canon G4, and are open to lay persons. Before such persons are appointed, the bishop or archbishop must be satisfied that the person to be appointed is a communicant. By implication (when read with

---

[112] Essays in Canon Law, A study of the law of the Church in Wales, edited by Norman Doe, at page 128, citing G.J. Cuming, The Durham Book (London, 1975), 229. See also Communion before Confirmation at page 63.

[113] I am informed by Mr Graham Phillips, formerly the diocesan secretary for Winchester, that after the Channel Islands were transferred from the diocese of Coutances first to the diocese of Salisbury and then to the diocese of Winchester in the 16th Century, the bishop of Winchester failed to pay them a visit for over 200 years! (For the Channel Islands forming part of the diocese of Winchester, see Halsbury's Laws of England 4th Ed., Vol. 14 paragraph 345, footnote 3).

[114] Canon C4

[115] Canon B23. "Nevertheless the minister shall have power to dispense with the requirement of confirmation in any case in which in his judgment need so requires" *ibid.* In practice, the first occasion when the minister meets the godparents or sponsors is likely to be the confirmation service itself, by which time it is rather late to get a replacement.

[116] Canon C4A

[117] Canon D2

[118] Canon E4

[119] Canon E7

Canon B15A) such a person must have been confirmed, or at least be ready and desirous of being confirmed.

To qualify to be on the electoral roll for a parish baptism is required, but confirmation is not[120]. Co-opted lay members of parochial church councils must be "an actual communicant as defined in rule 54 (1)"[121]. Rule 54 (1) provides that

> 'actual communicant' means a person who has received Communion according to the use of the Church of England or of a Church in communion with the Church of England at least three times during the twelve months preceding the date of his election or appointment being a person whose name is on the roll of the parish and is either
> (a) confirmed or ready and desirous of being confirmed; or
> (b) receiving the Holy Communion in accordance with the provisions of Canon B 15A paragraph 1 (b).

Similarly, churchwardens must be "actual communicant members of the Church of England except where the bishop shall otherwise permit"[122], and the same definition of "actual communicant member" applies[123].

Sidesmen must be on the electoral roll of the church[124], and must therefore be baptised, but need not be confirmed.

The qualifications required of a lay person for election by the diocesan electors of each diocese onto the House of Laity of General Synod is that

---

[120] Church Representation Rules (comprising Schedule 3 to the Synodical Government Measure 1969) Rule 1 (2) . The Rules are stated as at 1 January 1995, *i.e.* as amended most recently by the Church Representation Rules (Amendment) Resolution 1994 (S.I. 1994 No. 3118).

[121] Church Representation Rules, Rule 10 (1) (b)

[122] Churchwardens (Appointment and Resignation) Measure 1964 section 1

[123] Churchwardens (Appointment and Resignation) Measure 1964 section 13. Rule 1 of the Rules for the Representation of the Laity has been replaced by rule 44 of the Church Representation Rules: see Halsbury's Statutes 4th Ed., Vol. 14 page 70.

[124] Canon E2; Church Representation Rules, Rule 10 (2)

such person be an actual communicant[125], and therefore confirmed, or ready and desirous of being confirmed, or admitted under Canon B 15A paragraph 1 (b). Likewise a registered patron of a benefices, if not in holy orders, must either be a communicant, and therefore confirmed, or ready and desirous of being confirmed, or he must appoint someone else to carry out the functions of the patron[126].

There is no equivalent in the Church of England to Canon 1065 of the Catholic code, urging that engaged couples be confirmed before they are married in church[127]. But in the Book of Common Prayer, the rubric at the end of the service states

> It is convenient that the new married persons should receive the holy communion at the time of their Marriage, or at the first opportunity after their Marriage

which therefore assumes that the couple are both confirmed or ready and desirous of being confirmed. Similarly, the liturgies for the marriage service in the Deposited Book of 1928 and the Alternative Service Book both include communion as an option.

Baptism, rather than confirmation, is required for a Church of England burial[128]. The same is true in the Roman Catholic church.[129]

In the case of adults[130] who are to be baptised, the minister is under a duty to inform bishop at least a week before the baptism takes place[131]. The

---

[125] Church Representation Rules, rule 37 (1) (a).

[126] Patronage (Benefices) Measure 1986 sections 7 and 8

[127] *c.f.* Canons B30 – B36

[128] Canon B38

[129] Canon 1183 also permits catechumens a Catholic burial, and children whose parents intended to have them baptised but who died before baptism. Catechumens is understood as all those who have expressed in some way their desire to receive baptism, even though they have not been received formally into the catechumenate. See the Code of Canon Law Annotated edited by Caparros, Thériault and Thorn Caparros, Thériault and Thorn: Code of Canon Law Annotated, commentary on Canon 1183.

[130] Canon B24, par. 1: those "of riper years"

bishop is then under a duty to confirm the baptised person "so soon after his baptism as conveniently may be; that so he may be admitted to the Holy Communion"[132]

Likewise it is the duty of every minister who has a cure of souls diligently to seek out children and other persons whom he shall think meet to be confirmed and to use his best endeavour to instruct them in the Christian faith so that they can be.[133]

---

[131] Canon B24, par. 2

[132] Canon B24, par. 3

[133] Canon B27, par. 2. Compare Canon 890 of the Code of Canon Law.

Chapter Four

The proof and record of confirmation

The Roman Catholic Church

Because of the legal requirements for proof of confirmation in the circumstances given above[134], the Code prescribes that confirmations be noted in a register[135]. There is no requirement in the Code that a confirmed person be given a certificate of confirmation, and no reference to such a practice in the Rite of Confirmation itself. In practice however, a certificate of confirmation is almost invariably given[136]. Canon 241 § 2 refers to documents certifying baptism and confirmation; Canon 645 refers to "proof of baptism [and] confirmation", and in their notes to this Canon Coriden, Green and Heintschel refer to a confirmation certificate[137]. If juridical proof is required[138] it is rarely necessary to

---

[134] see chapter 3 above. Also, no doubt, partly for statistical reasons.

[135] Canon 895 provides that they be kept in a diocesan register. In England and Wales, the bishops have issued a complementary norm stating that in view of the long-established practice in England and Wales, a register of confirmation is to be kept in each parish rather than in a central register at the diocesan curia in accordance with Canon 895. See Caparros, Thériault and Thorn: Code of Canon Law Annotated, Appendix III, page 1335-1336.

[136] The standard certificates sold by St Paul Multimedia Productions UK cost 50 pence, and state as follows:

> ...... has received the Sacrament of Confirmation on ...... and was marked with the seal of the Holy Spirit in the Parish Community of
> ......

followed by the signature of the celebrant.

[137] Coriden, Green and Heintschel: The Code of Canon Law, A text and commentary, page 491.

[138] *semble* even the certificate of confirmation may be insufficient proof in nullity proceedings: *cp.* Coriden, Green and Heintschel: The Code of Canon Law, A text and commentary at page 630.

31

inspect the actual confirmation register: in these circumstances confirmations are proved by the confirmed person making a declaration[139].

The Church of England

As in the Roman Catholic church, confirmations are recorded in a register. These are kept in every parish[140]. There is no law requiring the minister or bishop to give to the confirmed person a certificate of confirmation, though this is the norm. Where proof of confirmation is required, the declaration of the confirmed person usually suffices[141].

---

[139] Canon 894 and Canon 876.

[140] Canon B39, par. 2, and Canon F11, par. 4

[141] *e.g.* a declaration under Patronage (Benefices) Measure 1986 section 8 that the person is "an actual communicant member of the Church of England or of a Church in communion with that Church". In many cases, *e.g.* the appointment of a churchwarden, not even a written declaration is required.

Chapter Five

The age for confirmation

*Then little children were brought to Jesus for him to place
his hands on them and pray for them. But the disciples
rebuked those who brought them. Jesus said, "Let the
little children come to me, and do not hinder them, for the
kingdom of heaven belongs to such as these." When he
had placed his hands on them, he went on from there*[142].

The Roman Catholic Church

In both the Roman Catholic church and the Church of England, baptism
must precede confirmation. Both churches have varying practices for the
age at which children who were baptised as infants are confirmed. Under
Canon 891 of the Catholic code, confirmation is to be conferred at about
the age of discretion, unless the Bishops' Conference has decided on a
different age, or there is a danger of death or, in the judgment of the
minister, a grave reason suggests otherwise. Children are presumed to
have the use of reason at the age of seven[143]. Therefore the standard age
for confirmation should be when a child is seven years old.

However this is not so in practice, and in many countries children receive
communion for years before being confirmed. In France, for example

> La confirmation est, en principe, le second des sacrements de
> l'initiation, après le baptême et avant l'eucharistie (can. 879-
> 896; rituel de 1971); mais en France, elle est généralement
> conférée après l'eucharistie, entre 12 et 18 ans. Pour les
> adultes, les trois sacrements du baptême, de la confirmation et
> de l'eucharistie sont administrés en même temps[144].

---

[142] Matthew 19:13-15.

[143] Canon 97 § 2

[144] *i.e.* "Confirmation is, in principle, the second of the sacraments of initiation,
after baptism and before holy communion; but in France, it is generally

The Catholic bishops' conferences in several English speaking countries have promulgated complementary norms on Canon 891. These suggest that confirmation is frequently deferred until the child is rather older than seven, so the Catholic and Church of England positions are closer than a first reading would suggest.

In Canada the conference of bishops decreed that the sacrament should be conferred "at the age determined in the approved catechetical programmes"[145]. In Gambia, Liberia, and Sierra Leone "it is left to the local diocesan bishop to decide the age at which confirmation is to be conferred". In India "As for the sacrament of confirmation, it can be conferred at a later age, say around 12-14 unless there is danger of death, or, in the judgment of the minister, a grave reason suggests otherwise". In Ireland

> In accordance with the prescription of c. 891, and in view of the long-established and pastorally successful practice in this country, the Irish Episcopal Conference hereby decrees that (apart from "a danger of death" or where "in the judgment of the minister a grave reason suggests otherwise") the sacrament of confirmation be conferred on the faithful not "at about the age of discretion", but rather towards the end of the primary-school education curriculum, *i.e.* at about the age of 11 or 12 years.

In Nigeria, the Catholic bishops' conference leaves the determination of age other than that of discretion for confirmation to the discretion of the local Ordinary. And in the Philippines:

> The age for the reception of the sacrament of confirmation throughout the country is *at least* seven years, or after the first

---

conferred after holy communion, between the ages of 12 and 18. For adults, the three sacraments of baptism, confirmation and holy communion are carried out at the same time". Jean Werckmeister: Petit Dictionnaire de Droit Canonique; Les Éditions du Cerf, Paris 1993, *sub nom* confirmation

[145] This, and the similar statements for the other countries quoted, from Caparros, Thériault and Thorn: Code of Canon Law Annotated, Appendix III.

34

communion, unless in the judgment of the minister a grave reason suggests otherwise.

As against this, it is worth noting that the following English speaking countries which have issued complementary norms to other Canons, have *not* issued complementary norms to Canon 891. These countries are Australia, England and Wales, Papua New Guinea and Solomon Islands, Scotland, and the United States of America[146]. However we cannot take the logical step of saying that therefore in these countries the age of seven is the norm. In Balhoff's article: Age for Confirmation: Canonical Evidence[147] at page 580 the author states[148] that many dioceses currently celebrate confirmation at a more mature age than seven, apparently without the norms from the Episcopal conference referred to in Canon 891, relying on the bishop's power to dispense with certain universal laws of the Church under Canon 87, § 1. Balhoff questions the legality of doing this habitually within a particular diocese, as dispensations under Canon 87, § 1 are not really intended to be used as an habitual avoidance of the universal law. Yet this appears to be the justification for the practice, *e.g.*, in America.

The position within England and Wales is summarised in On the Way paragraph 5.53

> Currently the practice varies in different dioceses in England and Wales. Thus Salford diocese encourages confirmation at 7 prior to first communion; Arundel and Brighton does not permit confirmation before children reach the age of 14.

---

[146] Caparros, Thériault and Thorn: Code of Canon Law Annotated, Appendix III, Footnote 1 states

> We communicated with the general secretaries of the bishops' conferences of countries partially or totally English-speaking. We reprint here the complementary norms as they have been published or forwarded to us. Most of the other [*semble* English-speaking] conferences have told us that they have not yet voted on complementary norms or, if so, that they have not yet received the recognitio from the Holy See.

[147] The Jurist, 45 (1985): 2, 549-587.
[148] The Jurist, 45 (1985): 2, 549-587 at page 580.

Balhoff argues that the central issue is not the age of confirmation, but rather that the three sacraments of baptism, confirmation and communion should together be seen as comprising initiation.

> The restoration of initiation based on the adult rite is one of the most important keys to understanding the postconciliar reform of baptism and confirmation.[149]

In the rite of adult initiation the adult is baptised, confirmed, and receives his first communion at the same service. At the other extreme, in the Russian Orthodox Church, the infant is baptised and confirmed and receives its first communion in a single service shortly after birth[150].

If emphasis is placed on the three sacraments separately, then two problems become apparent in the case of children who were baptised as infants and are confirmed later. First, the longer confirmation is deferred from baptism, the less it is seen as a sacrament of initiation. Second, the practice of admitting children to holy communion before they are confirmed, detracts from the holy communion being seen as the culmination of Christian initiation.

If, however, the emphasis is placed on seeing the three sacraments as parts of one whole, the order and sequence of the three sacraments assumes less importance. And this is the emphasis of Vatican II and the new Code.

The Church of England

The authors of the report Communion before Confirmation (1985) summarised the issue as follows:

> There are three clearly definable elements in Anglican Confirmation as received from earlier generations. They are:
> (a) Confirmation as admission to Communion.

---

[149] Balhoff, *op. cit.* at page 572.

[150] See Moore: Introduction to English Canon Law 3rd Ed. at page 64, and Caparros, Thériault and Thorn: Code of Canon Law Annotated at page 558

(b) Confirmation as ratification by an adult believer of baptismal vows made by proxy in infancy.

(c) Confirmation as the reception of the 'confirming' grace of the Holy Spirit.

The first two elements are contrary the one to the other in terms of the *age* for Confirmation: (a) is always trying to push the age down, as the desire to admit children to Communion bears upon it; (b) is always trying to push the age up, as the expectation that the candidate will be an adult believer requires an older age than the early teens to be credible.

Thus, the commonly found age of Confirmation in the Church of England, about 12 years, can be seen as an uneasy compromise between the conflicting principles, with the age veering up or down according to the relative force of these two principles in any particular parish.

...When Confirmation is required as a prerequisite for admission to Communion, it can assume the character of a 'leaving' certificate. This tends to imply that there is no need for further training and an individual's understanding of the Christian faith may remain fixed at that level. A more flexible approach, not requiring people to be confirmed before admission to Communion, could enable the development of more broadly based parish education programmes, for people of all ages.

In 1991 the General Synod published Martin Reardon's discussion paper Christian Initiation – A Policy for the Church of England[151]. Canon Reardon concluded[152]

Many in the Church of England (probably most) wish to retain: (a) *the traditional order* of infant baptism, confirmation on profession of faith (at puberty or shortly afterwards), followed by communion.

Others feel strongly that this is the wrong age for confirmation and blame the falling away of many young people from the Church at least partly on this pattern. Instead they propose either:

---

[151] Church House Publishing 1991 (GS Misc. 365)
[152] *op. cit.* paragraphs 133 – 135, at pages 49 – 50.

(b) the *Eastern pattern* of the baptism, chrismation and communion of infants, or

(c) *confirmation at a much earlier age* (perhaps seven years old), or else

(d) communion before confirmation.

There might be difficulties in allowing all four patterns to co-exist within the Church of England. However it would be wise at the beginning of a Decade of Evangelism to allow some flexibility, so that those who feel inhibited by the present pattern of initiation, and who are eager to explore the missionary, pastoral and educational possibilities of another pattern, may be free to use their skill and energy in doing so.

The Church should, under guidance from the House of Bishops, permit at least one other pattern in addition to what has become traditional. I believe they should permit either the Eastern pattern [*i.e.* (b)] ... *or* confirmation at a much earlier age than is at present usual in the Church of England [*i.e.* (c)]... If, however, they permit one or other of these options, then provision should be made for a personal profession of faith and act of commitment at a later age, perhaps in conjunction with admission to the electoral roll in a rite in which the candidate is admitted to the full privileges and responsibilities of adult membership of the Christian community.

If neither of these two options allowing confirmation or chrismation at a much earlier age were to commend itself, then communion before confirmation should be more widely permitted.

Canon Reardon, in the sentence immediately following the passage quoted above, says

Already more widespread use could be made of the rubric at the end of the Order of Confirmation in the Book of Common Prayer which allows those 'ready and desirous to be confirmed' to be admitted to receive communion.

The origin and scope of the phrase 'ready and desirous to be confirmed' has already been considered[153]. For the canon lawyer, the phrase does not

---

[153] see page 26 *supra*

seem a sufficient basis for permitting children to receive communion for several years before being confirmed. The regulations of the diocese of Oxford recognise one year as the period a person may be "ready and desirous".

> Young people who have reached puberty but are under the age of 18 years may be admitted to Communion before Confirmation, for a period of not more than one year, if in the opinion of the Minister-in-charge, they are ready and desirous to be confirmed. During this period they should be receiving instruction and the Area Bishop should be informed accordingly.

Diocesan Practice: age for confirmation

The minimum age for confirmation throughout the country varies from diocese to diocese. In several dioceses the regulations state that candidates below a certain age should not be presented for confirmation without the bishop's consent. These are as follows:

Diocese	Age below which the bishop's consent must be obtained
Birmingham	11
Blackburn	10
Bradford	12
Canterbury	12
Carlisle	12
Chelmsford	11
Chester	11
Chichester	10
Derby	12
Durham	10.5
Ely	11
Exeter	11
Guildford	12
Hereford	10
Lincoln	10
Lichfield	11
Liverpool	11

Diocese	Age below which the bishop's consent must be obtained
Manchester	11
Norwich	10
Oxford	7
Peterborough	12
Portsmouth	11
Ripon	11
Rochester	12
Southwark	10
Southwell	12
St. Edmundsbury and Ipswich	7
Truro	10
Winchester	11
Worcester	12
York	secondary school age

The diocese of Sodor & Man does not have, in any formal sense, laid-down regulations for the clergy, but

> I encourage instruction for Confirmation earlier rather than later, and am prepared to accept candidates as young as 9 years of age[154].

The following dioceses' regulations do not specify a minimum age for confirmation: Bath and Wells, Coventry, Gloucester, Leicester, London, Newcastle, Salisbury, St Albans and Wakefield. In Bristol

> I will not confirm under the age of 10 years. Encouragement is given to preparing young people when they are older than this[155].

Sheffield's regulations state

> There is no age restriction for those to be confirmed. However the Bishop expects the presenting incumbent to ensure that all

---

[154] letter from the Bishop of Sodor and Man to the author dated 7/3/95.
[155] letter from the Bishop of Bristol to the author dated 13/2/95. I have not seen any regulations, as such, for Bristol.

candidates are old enough to understand the meaning of their confirmation and baptismal promises, and to have an active commitment to Jesus Christ.

However to present the statistics[156] in this way is somewhat misleading. In many dioceses the regulations themselves recognise that confirmation may be appropriate at a lower age. The regulations for Carlisle, for example, state

> Normally candidates under the age of 12 may not be presented for Confirmation. There is, however, an increasing number of children for whom Confirmation below this age can be justified. Where the incumbent is satisfied that a child will benefit from Confirmation under the age of 12, he should ask for permission from the Bishop, giving the reasons. Such permission must be obtained *before* the preparation of the candidate begins. In every such case, the parents should be regular communicants, or else some other communicate member of the parish should make himself or herself responsible for the child.

In other cases, the age limit is seen as fairly inflexible. For example, in Durham:

> It is evident that there is much to be said for preparing children for Confirmation at an age before which, in many areas, they make the transition from primary to secondary education.
> With this in mind, the Bishop is prepared to allow candidates to be presented for Confirmation from the age of 10 years 6 months upwards. Permission for candidates to be presented under this age will only be given in exceptional circumstances and is subject in *every* case to permission being sought in writing from the Bishop at an early stage in the programme of preparation, in order to prevent disappointment if the request is not allowed.
> Clergy who present candidates under 12 years of age are particularly requested to assure themselves, as far as they are able, that the children concerned are capable or understanding

---

[156] It will be apparent from the above list that the only diocese about which I have not been able to obtain information is the diocese in Europe.

what they are undertaking and are made fully aware of their responsibilities.

Likewise in Canterbury

No candidate is to be presented under the age of 12 unless in exceptional circumstances by the special permission of the Bishop who is to take the Confirmation. This permission must be obtained at a very early stage of the preparation, and will not normally be given unless the incumbent from personal knowledge is convinced that the child understands the implications of the service, and is capable of making some real commitment of himself to Christ, and provided also that the child comes from a practising Christian background.

And in Lichfield

Incumbents who wish to present candidates at an earlier age than eleven must seek permission from the Diocesan or confirming bishop *before beginning to prepare them.* Permission will only be given in very exceptional circumstances.

Where children are to be presented for confirmation at a low age, the regulations frequently indicate the bishop's concern for after-care. In Derby, for instance,

The bishop requires, in the case of candidates under the age of 12, a personal assurance from the incumbent in writing, before the training of the candidate for Confirmation is begun, saying that he is convinced that earlier Confirmation is on special grounds desirable and, in particular, that the candidate will receive encouragement at home to persist in the communicant life.

Likewise, in Chichester,

There is no general rule concerning the age of candidates. Spiritual understanding is the most important criteria, and this may best be judged by those with immediate pastoral responsibility. Some Deaneries may feel it appropriate to hold separate Confirmations for children and adults.

In the case of children, account needs to be taken not only of their own level of understanding and devotion, but also of their home influences and environment. The Area Bishop should be consulted if children below 10 years of age are to be presented.

The regulations for Ripon state

Normally children under the age of 11 are not confirmed in the Diocese. The Bishops are willing to consider in certain circumstances confirming under this age, and indeed as young as 8. However the Bishops will need to be convinced that proper preparation for confirmation at this age has taken place and that there is a continuing scheme of nurture within the parish within which those confirmed at such a young age can be further prepared for Christian discipleship.[157]

In other cases the bishop's concern for after-care is not expressed in the regulations, but it is clear that this is a major factor in exercising his discretion in each case. Thus, in the case of Birmingham[158]

The Bishop is willing to confirm candidates who are younger than eleven, but he asks for consultation beforehand about this.
His usual practice is to allow the Confirmation of children under the age of eleven where the parish priest is clear that the child desires Confirmation, has reached a reasonable sense of discretion, and has the support of a faithful and practising home and family. Usually he prefers to give permission for a child younger than eleven to be confirmed rather than allowing a youngster to receive communion before Confirmation. The latter tends to blur the usual Church of England norm that Communion follows Confirmation.

---

[157] These regulations were issued in October 1990. In a letter from the Bishop of Ripon to the author dated 14/2/95 the Bishop stated that to date no request had been received for Confirmation under the age of ten.

[158] letter from the Bishop of Birmingham's chaplain to the author dated 30/1/95.

The Bishop of Chichester also insists on after-care for young children[159].

> I would be willing to confirm children at the age of seven, but if I were asked to do so I would make this conditional on some assurance of a proper system of training up to a much later age.

In the case of Newcastle, the Diocesan Information Book says

> it is left to the clergy to decide the age at which candidates are presented for Confirmation, and whether spiritually as well as intellectually the candidates have reached 'years of discretion'

The practice in the diocese is as follows:[160]

> Until recently it was generally understood that this ruling could include children of 10 years and upwards. However, since the last set of decisions by the House of Bishops concerning Christian Initiation I have let it be known that I am prepared to receive as candidates for confirmation children of 8 years old and upwards, provided that they come from church going families in which they will have encouragement and support.

again showing the importance of after-care. In the case of York the diocesan regulations state

> Only candidates of secondary school age may be presented unless the special permission of the Bishop who is to take the Confirmation has been obtained. Such permission should be asked for at least a month before the service.

The Archbishop's practice is[161]

> Twelve is now regarded as the normal minimum age, but candidates younger than that, even on occasions as young as nine, may be presented with special permission when the family circumstances warrant it.

---

[159] letter from the Bishop of Chichester to the author dated 30/1/95.

[160] letter from the Bishop of Newcastle to the author dated 26/1/95.

[161] letter from the Archbishop of York to the author dated 27/1/95.

In Oxford the age of seven is expressly mentioned in the diocesan regulations, and the issue of after-care is stressed.

> With the agreement of the Area Bishop (who should be consulted beforehand), children who have reached the age of seven years may be prepared and presented for Confirmation, provided that they will thereafter receive Holy Communion with their families (whether domestic or institutional) and are instructed in the Christian faith according to some definite plan.

In the diocese of Southwell

> There are of course numbers of cases where the Bishop exercises discretion to confirm under [the age of 12]. In the last six years there has been an experiment in one parish of children being confirmed at the age of seven.[162]

In the diocese of Worcester

> I am finding that an increasing number of children below the age of 12 are being presented for confirmation. Last year, out of a total of 825, 90 were under 12.[163]

In the diocese of Chelmsford

> where incumbents wish to present candidates under the age of eleven and over the age of eight (a) prior notice must be given, and permission sought of the confirming bishop; (b) there must be evidence of an ongoing programme of Christian education and nurture in the life of the parish, in which the child is known to be participating fully; (c) there must normally be support from the parents or sponsors of the child and a pattern of consistent worship at the eucharist or some other regular service; (d) the preparation must normally be done within a parish church setting rather than through a school so that the links for the child with the local worshipping community can be fostered. The continuing nurture of children by Word and Sacrament is of great importance, and care should be taken to

---

[162] letter from the Bishop of Southwell to the author dated 1/2/95.
[163] letter from the Bishop of Worcester to the author dated 10/2/95.

ensure that when they move elsewhere they are commended to the priest there.

Diocesan Practice: communion before confirmation

Oxford is also one of the dioceses which permit children to take communion before they are confirmed. The diocesan regulations state:

> The normal practice of the Church of England is to admit people to Communion only after they have been Confirmed. However, within the Anglican Communion as a whole many provinces admit children to Communion from a young age before they have been confirmed. Within the Church of England this possibility is the subject of recurrent debate, though the General Synod at the last opportunity rejected the idea of a change from present practice. As a contribution to the continuing debate on this subject particular parishes are allowed, under certain conditions, to admit children to Communion before Confirmation. A request for this should be made to the Area Bishop. It should come with the full endorsement of the Incumbent and PCC after a full debate on the subject. A preliminary code of practice should also be submitted. The Area Bishop will review the situation every three years, and may make use of an outside assessor. It must not be assumed that the change is permanent and the submission of a request cannot be taken as an indication that it will be automatically granted.

Similar regulations are in force for the dioceses of Southwark (for children from the age of seven), Winchester (for children from the age of eight), and in Manchester.

In the diocese of Peterborough

> baptised children aged eight and above are admitted to communion before confirmation at the request of their parish priest on condition that there is some course of nurture, training and encouragement for the children inside the life of the church, and that the child belongs either to a worshipping family or would be in a group of other youngsters who were

also coming forward. About 30 of the 365 parishes in the diocese permit children to take communion in this way[164].

In the diocese of St. Edmundsbury and Ipswich the bishop's regulations permit children to be confirmed from the age of seven, and for unconfirmed but baptised children to take communion from that age, subject to the bishop's consent being obtained.

> The chief factor which will need to be ensured is that children in either case are firmly held within a system of nurture in which they are both loved and affirmed and taught

In the diocese of Wakefield,

> We do have some parishes in which children are admitted to communion before confirmation on an experimental basis but since those few experiments were permitted years ago, there have been no fresh permissions and I detect that the practice is in retreat[165].

In the diocese of Southwell

> There are also in the region of ten parishes that are experimenting with Communion before Confirmation. In these parishes, guidance is given through our Board of Education and Children's Officer concerning the preparation of children for reception of Holy Communion. We are also monitoring these experiments to determine how many of these children do go forward to Confirmation. As yet, the experiments have not been running long enough for us to be able to have any reliable or firm statistics.[166]

In the diocese of Lincoln

> We have allowed admission to communion before confirmation on a limited and monitored basis, but this is a practice now questioned by the House of Bishops, and not encouraged.[167]

---

[164] letter from the Bishop of Peterborough to the author dated 2/2/95.

[165] letter from the chaplain to the Bishop of Wakefield to the author dated 2/2/95.

[166] letter from the Bishop of Southwell to the author dated 1/2/95.

[167] letter from the Bishop of Lincoln to the author dated 4/2/95.

In the diocese of Bath and Wells

> a handful of parishes were allowed to experiment in this way
> but the present Bishop is reluctant to extend this permission
> until there is a common mind amongst the Bishops[168].

In the diocese of Bristol

> There have been three experiments [of communion before
> confirmation] in this diocese for over fifteen years. All have
> been monitored. I have, in accordance with the decision of the
> House of Bishops not given permission for other experiments
> or for congregations to introduce communion before
> confirmation[169].

In the diocese of Guildford

> the new Bishop intends to implement a more flexible policy.
> More specifically, he intends to allow parishes to admit
> children to Communion before they are confirmed. At the
> moment it is difficult to say what this will mean for the age
> limit on confirmation. What the Bishop is clear about
> however, is that the changes he envisages will need to go hand
> in hand with parishes producing a far more coherent policy for
> the nurture and teaching of children.[170]

In 1993 the Culham College Institute[171] carried out research to evaluate
the experiments with communion before confirmation in the dioceses of
Manchester, Peterborough and Southwark. Its report states

> There was almost unanimous support among those who
> responded to the enquiry for the practice of admitting children
> to full participation in the Eucharist. While many recognised
> that there were some disadvantages or difficulties arising from
> it, very few indeed regarded these as outweighing the
> advantages. Several held such strong views on the subject that

---

[168] letter from the chaplain to the Bishop of Bath and Wells to the author dated 8/2/95.

[169] letter from the Bishop of Bristol to the author dated 13/2/95.

[170] letter from the Bishop of Guildford's chaplain to the author dated 20/3/95.

[171] Culham Educational Foundation, The Malthouse, 60 East St Helen Street, Abingdon, Oxon OX14 5EB.

they regarded it as unthinkable that they should revert to previous practice.

Respondents saw the main advantages as the benefits accruing to the children themselves, to their families and to the congregations as a whole. Most welcomed the enhanced significance they felt it gave to the rite of Baptism 'as full initiation into Christian privileges' and many also believed that it made Confirmation more meaningful as an adult profession of faith [172].

The verdict is not unanimous. But there is a very substantial majority, nearly four-fifths of all the parishes which responded to the present enquiry and virtually all of those involved fully in the experiment, which is convinced of the positive value of admitting children before Confirmation[173].

---

[172] Communion before Confirmation, Culham College Institute, at pages 32-33. See also On the Way, paragraphs 5.54 and 5.55.

[173] Communion before Confirmation, Culham College Institute, at page 34.

Chapter Six

Preparation for confirmation

The Roman Catholic Church

The Code of Canon Law requires that confirmation candidates be "properly instructed to receive the sacrament"[174] Likewise, in the case of adult baptism

> the celebration of baptism should be properly prepared. Accordingly, an adult who intends to receive baptism is to be admitted to the catechumenate and, as far as possible, brought through the various stages to sacramental initiation, in accordance with the rite of initiation as adapted by the Bishop's Conference and with the particular norms issued by it[175].

The Code does not say any more about the form the instruction is to take. The Rite of Christian Initiation of Adults describes in detail the rites of the catechumenate, the degrees it includes, and the internal dispositions it attempts to develop[176].

> The Catechumenate is an extended period during which the candidates are given suitable pastoral formulation and guidance, aimed at training them in the Christian life. In this

---

[174] Canon 890

[175] Canon 851

[176] Caparros, Thériault and Thorn: Code of Canon Law Annotated page 562 says "this has not been universally adopted". However On the Way paragraphs 3.6 to 3.14 gives a glowing tribute to the Rite:

> this rite has provided the norm for adult initiation in the Roman Catholic Church. It has contributed to radical change in Roman Catholic Church life in North America and Continental Europe. It has led to the flourishing involvement of lay people as catechists and sponsors for those coming to faith and to the development of extensive aids for catechumenal groups. ... Since the publication of an edition of the rites for England and Wales [it] is in use in virtually all dioceses.

way, the dispositions manifested at their acceptance into the catechumenate are brought to maturity.[177]

the time spent in the catechumenate should be long enough — several years if necessary — for the conversion and faith of the catechumens to become strong[178].

The origins of the catechumenate can be traced back to the third century, and the *Apostolic Tradition* of Hippolytus[179]. On the Way describes the Roman Catholic experience as follows:

it seems clear that its primary result has been to create a flexible framework in which individuals, with their experience and needs, are taken seriously and in which they can explore the faith and grow in a way that is properly supported and that goes at their own pace. Part of its attraction is undoubtedly that it does not strait-jacket people into a pre-ordained course but creates a spacious framework in which they can find their feet as Christians.[180]

The Church of England

According to the preface to the Order of Confirmation in the Book of Common Prayer, the Church of England

hath thought good to order, That none hereafter shall be Confirmed, but such as can say the Creed, the Lord's Prayer, and the Ten Commandments; and can also answer to such other Questions, as in the short Catechism are contained

Canon B27, paragraphs 2 and 3 provide

Every minister who has a cure of souls shall diligently seek out children and other persons whom he shall think meet to be confirmed and shall use his best endeavour to instruct them in

---

[177] The Rite of Christian Initiation of Adults paragraphs 75 - 80.

[178] The Rite of Christian Initiation of Adults paragraphs 76.

[179] See Christian Initiation, Birth and Growth in the Christian Society (The Ely Report), paragraph 82.

[180] On the Way paragraph 3.12.

the Christian faith and life as set forth in the holy Scriptures, the Book of Common Prayer, and the Church Catechism
The minister shall present none to the bishop but such as are come to years of discretion and can say the Creed, the Lord's Prayer, and the Ten Commandments, and can also render an account of their faith according to the said Catechism.

Canon B28, paragraph 2, concerns the reception into the Church of England of a person who has been baptised into some other church. It provides that such a person shall be formally admitted into the Church of England *after appropriate instruction* by the rite of confirmation[181].

Although most Christians can say the Lord's Prayer, and perhaps also a version of the Creed, from memory, learning the Ten Commandments and the Catechism by rote has fallen into desuetude. Most teaching which precedes confirmation is a general series of talks or discussions about the Christian faith, not necessarily all doctrinal. The requirements set out in the Book of Common Prayer are not included in the Alternative Service Book. However the candidates are required to give certain responses in the course of the service, and by implication the teaching preparatory to this service should cover the subject matter of these responses.

Question	*Response*
Do you turn to Christ?	I turn to Christ.
Do you repent of your sins?	I repent of my sins.
Do you renounce evil?	I renounce evil.
Do you believe and trust in God the Father who made the world?	I believe and trust in him.
Do you believe and trust in his Son Jesus Christ who redeemed mankind?	I believe and trust in him.
Do you believe and trust in his Holy Spirit who gives life to the people of God?	I believe and trust in him.

And it should be noted that Canon B27 distinguishes being able "to say the Creed, the Lord's Prayer, and the Ten Commandments" from being

---

[181] "or if he be not yet ready to be presented for confirmation, he shall be received by the parish priest with appropriate prayers"

able to "render an account of their faith according to the said Catechism". Thus, learning the Catechism by rote is not required, but *understanding* it is; and that is far more important[182].

The recent report On the Way recommends the preparation of a new Catechism:

> This needs to draw on the experience and needs of those coming to faith. The Group did not take the view that the New Revised Catechism would necessarily be the best starting point in such an endeavour. It would be best to continue the authorisation of the 1962 Revised Catechism for the time being, and to allow time for further consideration of the form of a catechism in the light of the Church's reception of this Report.[183]

On the Way also sees the catechumenate as a positive model for Christian initiation[184], and points to the part played by sponsors:

> An essential part of the Faith Journey as envisaged in the catechumenate is that it should be an accompanied one. The role of 'sponsor' is therefore highly significant. Essentially it is an Emmaus Road experience. The candidate and sponsor walk together. The sponsor - a lay person - cares for and prays for the candidate and introduces the candidate to the rites. The sponsor shares his own faith journey and helps the candidate to

---

[182] *cf.* Martin Bucer's criticism in the 16th Century of the mere recitation of certain formulae: "And it is evident that not a few children make a confession of this kind with not more understanding of the faith than some parrot uttering his Hallo.", cited in On the Way, paragraph 1.9. See also Bucer's Censura (1551), cited in Fisher J.D.C. Christian Initiation: The Reformation Period, pages 244-250 On the Way at paragraph 3.48 says:

> We recommend that the Lord's Prayer, the Apostles' Creed, Jesus' summary of the law, and the Beatitudes be available as texts which could be taken as liturgical focus for formation.

[183] On the Way, paragraph 6.11.

[184] On the Way sometimes limits the use of the term catechumenate to those who have not been baptised, *i.e.* to enquirers into the Christian faith, *e.g.* paragraph 3.5; at other times it encourages the use of the word 'enquirer' both for the baptised and the unbaptised, *e.g.* paragraph 3.34.

articulate and thus evaluate and value his own. In most circumstances sponsor and candidate are both members of a group. But the pattern also allows for, and gives space to, those who temperamentally are not group minded.[185]

Diocesan Practice

Many of the diocesan regulations refer to the importance of preparation, but most do so only in very general terms. Thus in the case of Bradford

> Methods of training should be devised not only to convey the facts of the Christian faith, but to involve learning for oneself and developing an eagerness to go on growing into Christian maturity.
> It will be a great help to know a little about the preparation for confirmation the candidates have received and outline details should be sent to the bishop.

In the case of Carlisle

> There should be careful preparation of the candidates, in which both Incumbent and members of the congregation should be involved.

In the diocese of Hereford

> Candidates should have regularly attended worship and have attended a course of instruction for at least four months.

Some dioceses are more specific. In the diocese of Southwark

> The greatest care should be taken over the preparation of candidates for Adult Baptism and Confirmation. No candidate should be presented to the Bishop until he or she has been thoroughly instructed in the basic Christian doctrines, in the use of scripture and in the practice of both corporate worship and personal prayer. The instruction should also include the implications of Christian belief on personal behaviour and social morality.

---

[185] On the Way paragraph 3.50; see also paragraph 8.4.

In the diocese of Birmingham

> The greatest care should be taken over the preparation of candidates for (Baptism and) Confirmation. The attention of Clergy is drawn to the content of the Catechism in the Book of Common Prayer and to the Revised Catechism (1962):
>
> Whenever it is possible and appropriate, lay people should be involved in the process of preparation. To be effective this requires careful selection, training and supervision.

And in the diocese of Sheffield

> Before candidates are presented for confirmation, there should have been a full course of instruction which each candidate has attended regularly. This course should cover some knowledge of the Scriptures, of the teaching of the Church, the responsibilities of church membership, and an encouragement of the candidates to live their lives in the love and obedience of Our Lord.

It is interesting to compare the time required in preparation as between the different dioceses. In Chelmsford, for example

> The bishops recommend that instruction will not normally be less than twelve weeks

Whereas in Salisbury

> It is appropriate, therefore, that the programme of confirmation preparation should extend over a period of one year leading up to the confirmation itself, and occupying, when allowance is made for breaks and holidays, not less than eight months of that time.
>
> Where candidates come forward for confirmation, or it seems pastorally right that they should be invited to do so, at times other than the beginning of a course, their period of instruction should not be reduced. If sufficient progress can be made by the time of the main confirmation, they may be presented then on condition that they finish their training afterwards. If this is not possible, they should complete their course and be presented elsewhere.

On the Way paragraph 1.13 refers to the Alpha course. The Alpha course was started by Holy Trinity, Brompton Road, London SW7 1JA, and is now in use in over twelve hundred churches. Alpha is a ten week course[186], and includes both video recordings and written material. It is aimed primarily at adults, although a Junior Alpha for younger people is in the course of preparation. It is not specifically designed as a confirmation course, rather as an introduction to the Christian faith for new Christians and for those thinking about the Christian faith. But it seems to me to be excellent material to use as part of the preparation for confirmation. And it is a testimony to the Grace of God; for many, many people have had their Christian lives strenghthened through it. For details, contact the Alpha office at Holy Trinity, Brompton: telephone 0171-581 8255.

---

[186] On the Way mistakenly refers to Alpha as a fifteen week course.

Chapter Seven

Who administers confirmation?

The Roman Catholic Church

The ordinary minister of confirmation is a bishop. A priest can validly confer this sacrament if he has the faculty to do so, either from the universal law or by way of a special grant from the competent authority.[187] Of particular interest is the faculty given to a priest who baptises one who is no longer an infant[188]. Under Canon 883 that priest has the faculty to administer confirmation. This faculty arises from the internal logic of the sacraments of Christian initiation, which recommends that confirmation be administered without delay to the adult who is being baptised[189]. The parish priest "or indeed any priest" has the faculty to confirm those in danger of death[190].

The Church of England

In the Church of England confirmation is administered by the bishop. Canon B27 paragraph 1 states

> The bishop of every diocese shall himself minister (or cause to be ministered by some other bishop lawfully deputed in his stead) the rite of confirmation throughout his diocese as often and in as many places as shall be convenient, laying his hands

---

[187] Canon 882

[188] *i.e.* someone who is aged seven or over: Canon 97 § 2

[189] Canon 863 On the Way at paragraph 3.11 describes the baptism and confirmation of catechumens:

> the candidates are baptised with great rejoicing during the Easter vigil. They are also confirmed during this rite and provision is made for their being confirmed by a priest if the bishop is not present.

[190] Canon 883 § 3

> upon children and other persons who have been baptised and instructed in the Christian faith.

Historically this seems to have taken place during the course of the bishop's visitation round his diocese[191]. Although the Book of Common Prayer and the Alternative Service Book both provide that another priest may assist in the service, it is only the bishop who may lay hands on the candidates[192].

One might ask why theologically the Church of England holds it necessary to have a bishop to administer the laying on of hands. Calvin considered confirmation could be administered by any presbyter[193]. For a scriptural precedent for confirmation *not* being administered by a bishop, see Acts 9:10-18[194], the story of Ananias laying hands on St. Paul[195]. It might be

---

[191] See Peter Smith: Points of Law and Practice concerning Ecclesiastical Visitations (1990-1992) 2 Ecc L.J. 189 at 201-2.

[192] The Book of Common Prayer refers to other ministers assisting (*e.g.* in saying the Preface). The Book of Common Prayer does not state expressly that only the bishop may confirm, but the rubric clearly states that it is the bishop who lays his hand on the candidates. In the Alternative Service Book this is expressly stated in the notes: "Delegation by the Bishop Where it is prescribed that anything is to be said or done by the Bishop, he may delegate it to other ministers; but only the Bishop is to confirm"

[193] J.D.C. Fisher: Christian Initiation: the Reformation Period, page 256.

[194] 10 In Damascus there was a disciple named Ananias. The Lord called to him in a vision, "Ananias!" "Yes, Lord," he answered.
11 The Lord told him, "Go to the house of Judas on Straight Street and ask for a man from Tarsus named Saul, for he is praying.
12 In a vision he has seen a man named Ananias come and place his hands on him to restore his sight."
13 "Lord," Ananias answered, "I have heard many reports about this man and all the harm he has done to your saints in Jerusalem.
14 And he has come here with authority from the chief priests to arrest all who call on your name."
15 But the Lord said to Ananias, "Go! This man is my chosen instrument to carry my name before the Gentiles and their kings and before the people of Israel.
16 I will show him how much he must suffer for my name."

argued that the significance of the bishop at the confirmation is that the bishop represents the wider church, and this symbolises that the candidate is a member of the whole body of Christ, not just a part of the local congregation.

On the Way also questions whether it is necessary for the bishop to confirm.

> ... it might be possible to follow the Roman Catholic practice of allowing presbyteral confirmation provided that the bishop was personally involved in at least *one* of the following ways:
> — presiding at the rite of call and decision in which a candidate was accepted for baptism, confirmation or reaffirmation.
> — involvement with the group during the extended period before baptism or related rite.
> — presided at a rite of welcome into episcopal communion in the period after a baptism or related rite.

---

17 Then Ananias went to the house and entered it. Placing his hands on Saul, he said, "Brother Saul, the Lord-- Jesus, who appeared to you on the road as you were coming here-- has sent me so that you may see again and be filled with the Holy Spirit."
18 Immediately, something like scales fell from Saul's eyes, and he could see again. He got up and was baptised,
[195] This laying on of hands was of course also before baptism. It also bears a similarity to the exorcism/healing which preceded baptism in the ancient rite, see the description of this rite in Cheslyn Jones: The Study of Liturgy, revised edition 1992 SPCK at pages 122 and 132.

Chapter Eight

After-care

The Roman Catholic Church

The Code of Canon Law provides that as far as possible the person to be confirmed is to have a sponsor. The sponsor's function is to take care that the person confirmed behaves as a true witness of Christ and faithfully fulfils the duties inherent in this sacrament[196]. Godparents have a similar role.

> Sponsors are persons who have known and assisted the candidates and stand as witnesses to the candidates' moral character, faith, and intention[197].
>
> Godparents ... continue to be important during the time after reception of the sacraments when the neophytes need to be assisted so that they remain true to their baptismal promises.[198]

These persons have a responsibility to provide Christian after-care, perhaps more important in the case of a child aged seven than for a grown up, but probably important for both.

The rite of confirmation describes the role of sponsors as follows:

> The candidate is presented to the bishop by the parish priest (or his representative) and by a sponsor. It is recommended that the sponsor should be one of the godparents; they made the act of faith and the promises when the little child took the first step towards entering the Church at baptism; it is appropriate that they should now present the candidate for the final stage of initiation. However, someone else (perhaps the parent) can perform this function, provided they are themselves confirmed Catholics and are sufficiently grown-up. The duty of the

---

[196] Canon 892
[197] Rite of Christian Initiation of Adults paragraph 10.
[198] Rite of Christian Initiation of Adults paragraph 11.

sponsor is not, as at baptism, to make the promises, for the candidate is now old enough to speak for himself. The priest and the sponsor represent the community that has introduced the candidate into the life of the Church, and now present him for a fuller share in that life.

The sponsor places his hand on the candidate's shoulder as a sign that he is presenting the candidate for confirmation on behalf of the whole congregation, the whole parish and the whole Church. He undertakes to encourage the candidate to fulfil his promise to be Christ's witness.

The key is in this last sentence. *"He undertakes to encourage the candidate to fulfil his promise to be Christ's witness"*. And in the general intercessions following the confirmation the same sentiment is expressed:

For their parents and godparents who led them in faith, that by word and example they may always encourage them to follow the way of Jesus Christ; let us pray to the Lord

The general statement of responsibility of sponsors in Canon 892 is parallel to what is said in Canon 872, in the case of baptism. It is elaborated upon in the *Roman Pontifical*

As a rule there should be a sponsor for each of those to be confirmed. These sponsors bring the candidates to receive the sacrament, present them to the minister for the anointing, and will later help them to fulfil their baptismal promises faithfully under the influence of the Holy Spirit whom they have received[199]

The Rite for Christian Initiation of Adults describes the period of post-baptismal[200] catechesis or mystagogy[201]

To strengthen the neophytes as they begin to walk in newness of life, the community of the faithful, their godparents, and

---

[199] *Ordo confirmationis*, Rite of Confirmation, Documents on the Liturgy 1963-1979, 2514, cited in Coriden, Green and Heintschel: The Code of Canon Law, A text and commentary page 641

[200] *i.e.* post-confirmation also

[201] The Rite of Christian Initiation of Adults paragraphs 244 - 251.

their parish priests (pastors) should give them thoughtful and friendly help.[202]

To close the period of post-baptismal catechesis, some sort of celebration should be held at the end of the Easter season near Pentecost Sunday[203].

On the anniversary of their baptism the neophytes should be brought together in order to give thanks to God, to share with one another their spiritual experiences, and to renew their commitment[204].

To show his pastoral concern for these new members of the Church, the bishop ... should arrange, if possible, to meet the recently baptized at least once in the year ...[205].

In these passages after-care is seen as the responsibility of the whole Christian community, including the bishop, the parish priest, sponsors, godparents, and all the faithful.

The Church of England

The Church of England encourages sponsors and godparents to attend the confirmation, but there is a common understanding that once the candidate has been confirmed, the duties of the sponsors and godparents are finished. The Church of England does not teach, regrettably, that sponsors and godparents should continue to encourage their charges even beyond confirmation. The only legal provision for after-care, if it may be called such, in the Church of England, is the duty[206] on all persons who have been confirmed to receive the Holy Communion regularly, and especially at the festivals of Christmas, Easter and Whitsun or Pentecost.

---

[202] The Rite of Christian Initiation of Adults paragraph 244.
[203] The Rite of Christian Initiation of Adults paragraph 249.
[204] The Rite of Christian Initiation of Adults paragraph 250.
[205] The Rite of Christian Initiation of Adults paragraph 251.
[206] Canon B15, par. 1

In Baptism and Confirmation Today, under the rubric Confirmation and After-Care, the report recommended

> Young men and young women who leave their parishes for service in the Forces, whether they are already confirmed, or are potential candidates for Baptism or Confirmation, should be commended to the Chief Chaplains of the respective Services[207].

John Stott in 1958[208] emphasised that growing as a Christian was primarily the responsibility of the person himself, rather than of the Christian community:

> We ministers are often to blame, I know. Sometimes we do not take the trouble we should in preparing you for confirmation. At other times we set you a poor example. We also do not pray for you as we should. Whether you continue to grow or not depends also on you, however. I would urge you to make up your mind to regard your confirmation as a beginning, not an end; as the first milestone, not the last; as the gateway to a new life, not a cul-de-sac which leads to nowhere....I hope you will be ...enthusiastic in regarding your confirmation only as the end of the beginning, and as the prelude to further victories in the service of your Captain, Jesus Christ. Post-confirmation listlessness is a common malady; be on your guard against it. When your confirmation is behind you, it is no time to sit back and rest on your oars. It is time rather to press ahead with vigour and determination.

However the Ely Report in 1971 recognised that the Church had an important part to play in after-care:

> Hitherto Confirmation has consisted of a rite, preceded by a course of instruction.

---

[207] National Service was still compulsory in 1954, so this recommendation would have affected quite a lot of people. The recommendation was adopted in May 1957 by the Convocations of Canterbury and York, each in Full Synod: see Smethurst, Acts of Convocation, page 156, or the 1971 edition by Riley and Graham at page 78. The recommendation is repeated verbatim in the diocesan regulations for Leicester.

[208] John Stott: Your Confirmation, page 39.

> We are suggesting that the development of the usual course of instruction into an on-going process of training which will meet the spiritual and intellectual needs of the individual and allow him to relate his experiences at every stage of growth to membership of the Church.   As the child passes into adolescence the Church will encourage and challenge him to grow up in faith and to assume a responsible role in the community[209].

It has already been seen that in most dioceses the regulations specify, or the diocesan practice is, for bishops only to confirm young children if satisfied that arrangements are in place for the child to receive after-care and support[210]. In very few dioceses do the regulations make any provision for after-care for other candidates. Manchester is one of the few who do.

> Parish priests should give candidates instruction appropriate to their age. It should be of at least three month's duration, and may continue after the confirmation.

In Lincoln

> My experience is that many clergy try to provide after-care but with limited (and mixed) success.[211]

On the Way[212] emphasises that after-care is the responsibility of the Church, at the parish, diocesan, national and ecumenical level.

> In the future much Christian learning must be based in congregations. ....Christian formation should not be limited to initial formation. ... There needs to be a willingness to think and act ecumenically ... Successful models of groups learning together keep a good balance between study and sharing of personal experience, individual and group activity, input and discussion, worship/prayer and social activity. ...The growing recognition of the role of the laity in leading 'enquirers' or

---

[209] Christian Initiation, Birth and Growth in the Christian Society (The Ely Report) paragraph 109.

[210] see diocesan practice: age for confirmation, page 39 *supra*

[211] letter from the Bishop of Lincoln to the author dated 4/3/95

[212] paragraph 4.34

nurture groups needs to be matched by a recognition of the importance of training and preparation, and of providing proper support structures at parish, deanery or diocesan level. Diocesan, national and ecumenical support agencies may be required.

Chapter Nine

Change of name at confirmation

The Roman Catholic Church

Canon 855 deals with the Christian name which may be given to a person at his baptism.

> Parents, sponsors and parish priests are to take care that a name is not given which is foreign to Christian sentiment.

There is no provision under the Code for a candidate's Christian name to be changed at confirmation. Nor is there any reference to such a practice in the Rite of Confirmation. The Rite of Christian Initiation of Adults[213] has an optional rite for the giving of a new name as part of the rite of acceptance into the order of catechumens, but catechumens are persons who have not been baptised. The second step of the catechumenate is the rite of election or enrolment of names, but this contains no provision for a name to be changed[214]. There is a rite of choosing a *baptismal* name[215], but no similar rite for the choosing of a name at confirmation[216]. The Rite of Christian Initiation of Adults also contains various other "rites for particular circumstances"[217], but none of these refer to the giving of a new name at confirmation[218].

---

[213] The Rite of Christian Initiation of Adults at paragraph 73.

[214] The Rite of Christian Initiation of Adults at paragraphs 129 ff.

[215] The Rite of Christian Initiation of Adults at paragraph 200. The readings suggested for use at the rite are

[216] The Rite of Christian Initiation of Adults, paragraphs 231 - 235.

[217] *i.e.* (1) Christian initiation of children who have reached catechetical age, (2) Christian initiation of adults in exceptional circumstances, (3) Christian initiation of a person in danger of death, (4) Preparation of uncatechized adults for confirmation and eucharist, and (5) Reception of baptized Christians into the full communion of the Catholic Church.

[218] see *e.g.* The Rite of Christian Initiation of Adults at paragraphs 322 - 326; 362 - 366; 388 - 391; 492 - 494;

According to Halsbury, an addition to the baptismal name at confirmation is usual in the Roman Catholic Church[219]. My informal conversations with Catholics show that many Catholics do adopt an additional name on confirmation, and that the practice is more common than in the Church of England.

For the theology of giving a new name, see the Rite of Christian Initiation of Adults paragraph 201[220], and Genesis 17: 5[221], Isaiah 62:4[222], Revelation 3:12[223], Matthew 16:18[224], and John 1:42[225].

---

[219] Halsbury's Laws of England 4th Ed. Vol. 35 paragraph 1273 footnote 3

[220] For a historical account of how the giving of a Christian name came to be associated with baptism, see J.D.C. Fisher: Christian Initiation: Baptism in the Medieval West pages 149-157.

[221] 5   No longer will you be called Abram; your name will be Abraham, for I have made you a father of many nations.

[222] 4   No longer will they call you Deserted, or name your land Desolate. But you will be called Hephzibah, and your land Beulah; for the LORD will take delight in you, and your land will be married.

[223] 12   Him who overcomes I will make a pillar in the temple of my God. Never again will he leave it. I will write on him the name of my God and the name of the city of my God, the new Jerusalem, which is coming down out of heaven from my God; and I will also write on him my new name.

[224] 18   And I tell you that you are Peter, and on this rock I will build my church, and the gates of Hades will not overcome it.

[225] 42   And he brought him to Jesus. Jesus looked at him and said, "You are Simon son of John. You will be called Cephas" (which, when translated, is Peter).

The Church of England

The term "Christian name" is found in the Companies Act 1985, sections 289, 290 and 305, and in the Marriage Act 1949, section 8. Neither statute defines the term Christian name (though the Companies Act 1985 specifies that "Christian name" includes a forename), but the proper meaning of the term is the name given at baptism. Thus, in Coke's Institutes, Christian name and baptismal name are treated as synonymous.

> And regularly it is requisite, that the purchaser be named by the name of baptism and his surname, and that speciall heed bee taken to the name of baptism; for that a man cannot have two names of baptism as he may have divers surnames. ......
> And this doth agree with out ancient books, where it is holden that a man may have divers names at divers times, but not divers Christian names.[226]

Since at least the time of Lord Coke in the sixteenth century it has been established that a person may change his name at confirmation. To quote Vaisey J. in *Cox v Parrott* [1946] Ch. 183 at page 186:

> There are only two, or at most three, ways in which a Christian name may be legally changed. Firstly, it may be assumed, by the omni-competence of an Act of Parliament, as for example, the Baines Name Act, 1907. Secondly, at confirmation, as explained in Phillimore's Ecclesiastical Law, 2nd ed., Vol. 1., at p. 517, where the following passage from Coke's Institutes 1., 3a, is cited: "If a man be baptized by the name of Thomas, and, after, at his confirmation by the bishop, he is named John, he may purchase by the name of his confirmation".

(The third possible way referred to by Vaisey J. is under the power to "add" a name when a child is adopted.)

Canon B27 paragraph 6 states:

> If is desired for sufficient reason that a Christian name be changed, the bishop may, under the laws of this realm, confirm a person by a new Christian name, which shall be thereafter deemed the lawful Christian name of such person.

---

[226] Coke's Institutes 1., 3a

A record of the change of name must be made in the register book of confirmations (Canon B39, paragraph 2).

In Legal Opinions Concerning the Church of England, the Legal Advisory Commission advise:

> Because the actual Christian name in use and that in the baptismal register (and on the birth certificate) will be different, it is advisable, though strictly unnecessary, that a statutory declaration should also be made in order to evidence the change of name. It is also advisable that a note of the change of name should be made in the margin of the baptismal register, although the register itself may not be altered.

The regulations for the dioceses often contain instructions on what is to be done when a candidate wishes to change his name at confirmation. Two examples will suffice. In the diocese of Chichester

> If a candidate wishes to take an additional Christian name at the time of Confirmation the Bishop should be informed and the candidate will be confirmed under this name as well as the one normally used if they are different. A statement to the effect that this has been done must be prepared for the Bishop to sign.

In the case of Peterborough, the regulations state that the bishop will need to know in advance of any change of name, the advice given by the Legal Advisory Commission is summarised, and the regulation concludes:

> The Bishop advises that clergy should discourage the taking of extra names as it will mean a lot of work for the candidate's family.

Strictly, there is no right for a person to change his name at confirmation, but a power given to the bishop to confirm a person by a new name. As Vaisey J. stated in *Cox v Parrott* [1946] Ch. 183 at page 187:

> The bishop's power is discretionary, and is only exercised for what he regards as a good and sufficient reason.

Clearly a refusal by the bishop would be justified if the new Christian name were offensive. If the bishop did refuse, and the candidate wished to change his Christian name none the less, the appropriate method[227] appears to be by deed poll, which may be enrolled in the Central Office of the Supreme Court pursuant to R.S.C. Order 63 rule 10. In such cases a certificate must be filed to the following effect:

> Notwithstanding the decision of Vaisey J. in *Re Parrott, Cox v Parrott* [1946] Ch. 183, the applicant desires the enrolment to proceed [228].

The efficacy of this procedure must therefore be somewhat doubtful.

---

[227] Not many people would wish to go to the trouble of a private Act of Parliament.

[228] Halsbury's Laws of England 4th Ed., Vol. 35, paragraph 1273, footnote 8

Chapter Ten

Confirmation and church membership

The Roman Catholic Church

Membership of the church begins at baptism. Canon 96 provides:

> By baptism one is incorporated into the Church of Christ and is
> constituted a person in it with duties and rights which are
> proper to Christians, in keeping with their condition, to the
> extent that they are in ecclesiastical communion and unless a
> legitimately issued sanction stands in the way.

Likewise Canon 204 provides

> The Christian faithful are those who, inasmuch as they have
> been incorporated in Christ through baptism, have been
> constituted as the people of God; for this reason, since they
> have become sharers in Christ's priestly, prophetic and royal
> office in their own manner, they are called to exercise the
> mission which God has entrusted to the Church to fulfil in the
> world, in accord with the condition proper to each one.
> This Church, constituted and organised as a society in this
> world, subsists in the Catholic Church, governed by the
> successor of Peter and the bishops in communion with him.

Baptism thus has a sacramental and a juridic effect: sacramental
incorporation into the Church, and a juridical bestowal of rights and
duties. As Coriden, Green and Heintschel state[229]:

> Canon 204 describes who are Christian faithful. Baptism is
> fundamental to being a Christian faithful, and by it one is
> incorporated into Christ and into Christ's Church, with the
> rights and duties that pertain to those who are in the Church.
> This description fits any baptised person, but in the context of

---

[229] Coriden, Green and Heintschel: The Code of Canon Law, A text and
commentary, page 125

what is enforceable under the Code it pertains to Catholics in general and to Latin Rite Catholics in particular.

Thus, in law, a member of the Catholic Christian faithful is called to participate in the Church's mission, exercising the threefold functions of teaching, sanctifying, and ruling by which the people of God — the Church — continue Christ's mission. ...Such participation in the church's mission for a Catholic is within the context of the Catholic Church in which the Church of Christ subsists.

The rights and duties of the baptised are mainly to be found in book II of the Code: The People of God; and specifically in Canons 208 to 231. Adopting Coriden, Green and Heintschel's summary at page 136

The list seems to have the following organisation. First come four statements relative to the basic equality of Christians — equality, communion, universal call to holiness, and participation in the mission of the Church (cc. 208-211). Next are obligations and rights that arise from the hierarchical differentiation in the church — obedience, petition, and public opinion (c.212). The means of sanctification are addressed, including the rights to spiritual goods, to worship according to an approved rite, and to a personal spirituality in keeping with church teaching (cc. 213-214). Four statements relative to the mission of the Church follow — rights to association and assembly, apostolic works, education, and freedom of inquiry and expression in sacred studies (cc. 215-218). Personal rights are listed — freedom from coercion in choosing a state in life, good name, and privacy (cc.219-220). One canon lists three basic protections or rights — vindication of rights, due process in court, and legality of penalties (c. 221). Finally certain social relationships are specified — support for the Church, promotion of social justice, aid to the poor, respect for the common good, and limitations on rights in virtue of the common good (cc. 222-223).

Rights specific to various groups in the church are also listed. For lay persons, canons 225-231 list seven obligations and rights as well as six capacities recognised in law. The obligations and rights concern participating in the mission of the Church, the vocation of married persons, duties of parents, Christian education, higher theological education, formation for church service, and a just family wage and benefits when employed in church service. Capacities relate to the functions of teaching (a mandate to teach theology), of sanctifying (installed ministries, temporary deputation for liturgical service, and supplying for services of ministers), and of ruling (assignment to church office, service as consultants). Lay persons are explicitly acknowledged to enjoy the obligations and rights of all Christian faithful; this list is considered a further specification in light of their situation in life (c. 224).

All this stems from baptism. Confirmation has no juridical connection with church membership. Though it is noteworthy that it is expressly mentioned in Canon 225, in connection with the duty of mission.

Since lay people, like all Christ's faithful, are deputed to the apostolate by baptism and confirmation, they are bound by the general obligation and they have the right, whether as individuals or in associations, to strive so that the divine message of salvation may be known and accepted by all people throughout the world. This obligation is all the more insistent in circumstances in which only through them are people able to hear the Gospel and to know Christ.

Nor is the continuing obligation to go to Mass linked with confirmation. Canon 920 provides

Once admitted to the blessed Eucharist, each of the faithful is obliged to receive holy communion at least once a year.

This Canon applies to all baptised persons who have been admitted to communion, which therefore includes children who have not been confirmed.

Chapter Ten

The Church of England

Judicial definitions of church membership

A useful starting point[230] is that of Stirling J. in *re Perry Almshouses*
[1898] 1 Ch. 391. Stirling J. stated at page 400 as follows:

> Whatever difficulty there may be in giving a strict legal
> definition of what constitutes membership of the Church of
> England, I think that a person who has been baptised, has been
> confirmed, or is ready and desirous to be confirmed, and is an
> actual communicant, does hold the status of a member of that
> Church, and would be ordinarily regarded and spoken of as
> such.

His judgment was upheld in the Court of Appeal: [1899] 1 Ch. 21.

In *re Allen* [1953] Ch. 810 a testator devised certain freeholds to the
eldest of the sons of his nephew F "who shall be a member of the Church
of England and an adherent to the doctrine of that Church", with a gift
over. The Court of Appeal held that the gift was not void for uncertainty.
All three Lords Justices approved the passage quoted from *re Perry
Almshouses*. Birkett L.J. remarked at page 827

> The Church of England is an institution bound into the
> national life by a thousand links, legal and historical. It seems
> to me to be a very strange conclusion that when millions of
> people, drawn to that Church by ties of piety, or feeling, or
> history, claim to be and are recognised to be members of that
> Church, this court should say that the words employed by this
> testator are so uncertain in their meaning as to be void, and the
> beneficiary is not even entitled to try to show that he occupies a
> position that millions of his countrymen enjoy without any
> question being raised.

Some further guidance can be found in the subsequent history of *re Allen*.
In *re Allen (No 2)* [1954] Ch. 259 at page 264 Harman J. refers to the

---

[230] cited in Halsbury's Laws of England 4th Ed., Vol. 14 paragraph 346
footnote 2.

concept of "formal membership" by baptism and communion. He says as follows:

> ...that suggests a living person of whom the trustees can inquire as to the state of his belief both formally and spiritually; that is to say, they must find out whether he is formally a member of the Church by baptism and Communion, and, second, whether his adherence to the doctrine of the Church is sincere.

A gloss on the definition of membership is found in *Marshall v Graham* [1907] 2 K.B. 112 at 124. The case concerned a parent withdrawing his child from school on Ascension day to attend church.

> The other finding of the justices upon which the conviction in Bell's case was based is to my mind a very extraordinary one. We have not heard any argument from Mr Dankwerts upon it. The man said he was a member of the Church of England; he had been baptised and confirmed according to the rites of that Church. He had previously to his marriage attended church regularly. Since 1895 he had only attended twice, once on his wedding day and once on the occasion of a funeral. Upon this evidence the justices said that they were not satisfied that the appellant bona fide belonged to the Church of England. I think it would be very improper to hold that, because a man had been irregular in his attendance at church, he did not honestly belong to the religious body of which he claimed to be a member.

So, regular attendance is not necessary for church membership; though according to Stirling J., a person who *is* an actual communicant and is baptised and confirmed into that Church is clearly a member of it.

The Canons of the Church of England

There are only a few references to membership in the Canons. More often the Canons refer to baptised persons, or to persons who have been confirmed, as the subject of a particular right or duty.

Canon A1 provides:

> The Church of England, established according to the laws of this realm under the Queen's Majesty, belongs to the true and apostolic Church of Christ; and, as our duty to the said Church of England requires, we do constitute and ordain that *no member thereof* shall be at liberty to maintain or hold the contrary.

Canon A2 provides

> The Thirty-nine Articles are agreeable to the Word of God and may be assented unto with a good conscience by *all members of the Church of England.*

Canon A3 (Of the Book of Common Prayer) provides

> The form of God's worship contained in the said Book, forasmuch as it is not repugnant to the Word of God, may be used by all *members of the Church of England* with a good conscience.

The duties of church members

Canon B15 provides:

> It is the duty of all who have been confirmed to receive the Holy Communion regularly, and especially at the festivals of Christmas, Easter and Whitsun or Pentecost.

Canon B29 points out

> It is the duty of *baptised persons* at all times to the best of their understanding to examine their lives ... and to bewail their own sinfulness and to confess themselves to Almighty God with full purpose of amendment of life, that they may receive of him the forgiveness of their sins

There is no reference here to membership or to confirmation: the duty is on all baptised persons.

In October, 1953 the following statement of the obligations of church membership was adopted by the two Houses of Canterbury and by the Convocation of York, in Full Synod.

The duties of church membership

Drawn up by the Convocation at the request of the House of Laity of the Church Assembly.

1. To pray every day and to read the Bible regularly.
2. To join in the worship of the Church every Sunday, and to observe Holy Days.
3. To receive the Holy Communion regularly after due preparation, and more particularly at the great Festivals of the Church and on the great occasions of their own lives.
4. To mark Fridays, and the season of Lent, by special acts of devotion and self-denial.
5. To contribute worthily to the work of the Church at home and overseas, and for the relief of those in need.
6. to uphold the marriage laws of the Church, and to bring up children to love and serve the Lord.

These rules do not attempt to cover the whole of Christian life and conduct. They assume that every Churchman loyally endeavours to follow the example of our Saviour Christ; to play his full part in the life and witness of the Church; and to give Christian service to his neighbours and community. They spring from the teaching of the Prayer Book; and while they do not include all the duties of man as set forth in the Church Catechism, they nevertheless are duties which loyal members of the Church of England should include in their personal rule of life.[231]

---

[231] printed in Smethurst and Wilson: Acts of the Convocations of Canterbury and York, page 173, or Riley and Graham at page 132.

In May 1954 it was announced in Full Synod that there would shortly be published: "A Short Guide to the Duties of Church Membership. Issued by the Archbishops of Canterbury and York at the request of the Church Assembly". This summary of the duties of church membership for persons who have been baptised and confirmed is set out below[232].

A short guide to the duties of church membership

All baptised and confirmed members of the Church must play their full part in its life and witness. That you may fulfil this duty, we call upon you:

To follow the example of Christ in home and daily life, and to bear personal witness to Him.

To be regular in private prayer day by day.

To read the Bible carefully.

To come to church every Sunday.

To receive the Holy Communion faithfully and regularly.

To give personal service to Church, neighbours and community.

To give money for the work of parish and diocese and for the work of the Church at home and overseas.

Geoffrey Cantuar:
Cyril Ebor:
1954

It is perhaps surprising that the short guide does not include the requirement to uphold the marriage laws of the Church, and to bring up children to love and serve the Lord. The practice of marking Fridays, and the season of Lent, by special acts of devotion and self-denial, is less common in 1995 than it was forty years ago, and so this omission in the short guide is less important than it may have been in 1954.

---

[232] reprinted in John Stott: Your Confirmation, Hodder and Stoughton 1958 page 117.

Either the short guide or the full list should I consider be incorporated in the canons. The canons are not of their own force binding on the laity[233], and it could be said that the statements in these Guides are too vague to be enforceable in the ecclesiastical courts in any event. But whichever version was incorporated in the canons would thereby achieve more publicity, and confirmed members of the Church of England would be encouraged to live their lives in accordance with it.

---

[233] Halsbury's Laws of England 4th Ed., Vol. 14 paragraph 308, and the cases mentioned there.

Chapter Eleven

Confirmation in ecumenical relations

The Roman Catholic Church

Ecumenical relations generally

The ecumenical movement is the impetus to restore unity among all Christians[234]. The church is bound by the will of Christ to promote that unity[235]. The college of bishops and the Holy See are to direct the participation of Catholics in the ecumenical movement, and the bishops are to do the same in the churches entrusted to them[236].

There is no legislation as such promulgated by the Roman Catholic Bishops of England and Wales for local ecumenical activity[237], though some important statements have been made on the subject. In particular, in 1979 the then Ecumenical Commission of England and Wales published *Local Covenants*, in which churches were encouraged to pledge themselves to

> joint prayer and worship
> support of others in maintaining their own traditions;
> dialogue;
> co-operation in domestic ministry;

---

[234] Coriden: An Introduction to Canon Law, Paulist Press, New York 1991, page 105.

[235] John 17:20-21
20 My prayer is not for them alone. I pray also for those who will believe in me through their message,
21 that all of them may be one, Father, just as you are in me and I am in you. May they also be in us so that the world may believe that you have sent me.

[236] Canon 755.

[237] see Ecumenical Relations, Canons B43 and B44: Code of Practice, page 37, and Caparros, Thériault and Thorn: Code of Canon Law Annotated, page 1336.

> joint pastoral care of interchurch families;
> working as a team in mission;
> exploration of joint evangelism;
> co-operation in the Christian education of those at school and of adults[238]

In 1983 the Ecumenical Commission published *Local Churches in Covenant*, with the approval of the Roman Catholic Bishops of England and Wales, which developed further the ideas contained in *Local Covenants*, and the theology underpinning them.

Sharing in sacraments

The Roman Catholic Church does not admit to Holy Communion Christians who have been confirmed (or even just baptised) in the Church of England, unless they have thereafter been received into the Roman Catholic Church, or unless one of the exceptional circumstances set out in Canon 844 applies.

Canon 912 provides that any baptised person who is not prohibited by law can and must be admitted to Holy Communion. But this is limited to persons who are baptised in the Roman Catholic Church or received into it. Canon 11 provides

> Merely ecclesiastical laws bind those who were baptised in the catholic church or received into it, and who have a sufficient use of reason and, unless the law expressly provides otherwise, who have completed their seventh year of age

Canon 844 sets out the general rule that Roman Catholic ministers may lawfully administer the sacraments only to Roman Catholic faithful, who, in their turn, may only receive them lawfully from Roman Catholic ministers.

> §1. Catholic ministers may lawfully administer the sacraments only to catholic members of Christ's faithful, who equally may

---

[238] see Ecumenical Relations, Canons B43 and B44: Code of Practice, pages 37-38

lawfully receive them only from catholic ministers, except as provided in §§ 2, 3 and 4 of this canon and in Canon 861 § 2[239]

§2 Whenever necessity requires or a genuine spiritual advantage commends it, and provided the danger of error or indifferentism is avoided, Christ's faithful for whom it is physically or morally impossible to approach a catholic minister, may lawfully receive the sacraments of penance, the Eucharist and anointing of the sick from non-catholic ministers in whose Churches these sacraments are valid.

§3 Catholic ministers may lawfully administer the sacraments of penance, the Eucharist and anointing of the sick to members of the eastern Churches not in full communion with the catholic Church, if they spontaneously ask for them and are properly disposed. The same applies to members of other Churches which the Apostolic See judges to be in the same position as the aforesaid eastern Churches so far as the sacraments are concerned.

§4 If there is a danger of death or if, in the judgement of the diocesan Bishop or of the Bishops' Conference, there is some other grave and pressing need, catholic ministers may lawfully administer these same sacraments to other Christians not in full communion with the catholic Church, who cannot approach a minister of their own community and who spontaneously ask for them, provided that they demonstrate the catholic faith in respect of these sacraments and are properly disposed.

§5 In respect of the cases dealt with in §§ 2, 3 and 4, the diocesan Bishop or the Bishops' Conference is not to issue general norms except after consultation with the competent authority, at least at the local level, of the non-catholic Church or community concerned.

---

[239] Canon 861 § 2 contemplates the giving of baptism by "any person with the right intention in case of necessity".

As the Ecumenical Relations, Canons B43 and B44: Code of Practice states[240]:

> It must be noted that the sharing in prayer and worship which Roman Catholics are urged to undertake with their fellow Christians does not include sacramental sharing. The RC bishops ...point out that occasional exceptions are made in the form of individual admissions to holy communion, but the general laws remain in force.

Recognition of Church of England confirmation

The reception of a non-Catholic baptised Christian into the Roman Catholic church recognises the validity of that person's baptism[241]. Canon 869 provides

> Those baptised into a non-catholic ecclesial community are not to be baptised conditionally unless there is a serious reason for doubting the validity of their baptism, on the ground of the matter or the form of words used in the baptism, or of the intention of the adult being baptised or that of the baptising minister.

The Code says nothing about the validity of any previous sacrament of confirmation which such persons may have received in their previous church. Repetition of confirmation is forbidden, in the same way as repetition of baptism is forbidden[242]. But as the Roman Catholic Church does not recognise Anglican orders, the Roman Catholic Church does not recognise the validity of a Church of England confirmation. The form of reception provides

> if the person being received has not yet received the sacrament of confirmation, the celebrant lays hands on the candidate's

---

[240] at page 38

[241] see the principles expressed in the Forward and Introduction to the *Rite of Reception of Baptised Christians into Full Communion with the Catholic Church* (Washington: United States Catholic Conference) pages 1-7

[242] Canon 845 and Canon 889

head and begins the rite of confirmation with the following prayer ...[243]

This part of the liturgy is always included when a Church of England member is received into the Roman Catholic Church. Likewise the requirement of confirmation as a condition for admission to a religious institute or seminary, or for ordination[244], would be satisfied not by a Church of England confirmation, but by the confirmation received when the person is received into the Roman Catholic Church.

Ecumenical confirmation celebrations

There is no provision in regulations issued by the Roman Catholic Bishops (nor in the Code itself) for joint Roman Catholic and Church of England confirmation services. Canon 844 refers only to the sacraments of penance, the Eucharist and the anointing of the sick. Thus it does not authorise Roman Catholics to be confirmed other than by a Roman Catholic minister or bishop[245].

The Church of England

Ecumenical relations generally

> The Church of England is committed to the search for full, visible unity with other Christian Churches, and to the bodies which promote this at the local, intermediate, national, European and World levels.[246]

Canon B43 (Of Relations with Other Churches) and Canon B44 (Of Local Ecumenical Projects) encourage and make provision for sharing in worship with other Churches. Full details are given in The Ecumenical Relations Code of Practice. The Roman Catholic Church in England and

---

[243] Rite of Christian Initiation of Adults paragraph 493.

[244] see Chapter 3 above.

[245] *i.e.* in accordance with Canon 882.

[246] The Church of England Yearbook 1995 page 333.

Wales is one of the Churches designated by the archbishops of Canterbury and York as Churches to which the Church of England (Ecumenical Relations) Measure 1988, and thus Canon B43 and Canon B44 apply[247].

Sharing in sacraments

Canon B15A paragraph 1 provides

> 1. There shall be admitted to the Holy Communion
> (a) members of the Church of England who have been confirmed in accordance with the rites of that Church or are ready and desirous to be so confirmed or who have been otherwise episcopally confirmed with unction or with the laying on of hands except as provided by the next following Canon.
> (b) baptised persons who are communicant members of other Churches which subscribe to the doctrine of the Holy Trinity, and who are in good standing in their own Church.
> (c) any other baptised persons authorised to be admitted under regulations of the General Synod; and
> (d) any baptised person in immediate danger of death.

Under paragraph (b) of these provisions, it is clear that communicant Roman Catholics, who are in good standing in the Roman Catholic Church, are admitted to Holy Communion in the Church of England. This is intended as a temporary privilege, not to continue indefinitely. Canon B15A paragraph 2 provides

> If any person by virtue of sub-paragraph (b) above regularly receive the Holy Communion over a long period which appears likely to continue indefinitely, the minister shall set before him the normal requirements of the Church of England for communicant status in that Church.

The assumption in Canon B15A paragraph 2 is that episcopal confirmation is "the normal requirement" for communicant status[248].

---

[247] see The Church of England Yearbook 1995 page 333.
[248] see On the Way paragraph 4.56.

Recognition of Roman Catholic confirmation

Canon B15A is not a recognition of confirmation in the Roman Catholic Church, as the Roman Catholic Church does not limit communion to persons who have been confirmed. Nor is Rule 54 (1) (b) of the Church Representation Rules a recognition of Roman Catholic confirmation. Both these provisions are a recognition by the Church of England only of communicant status in the Roman Catholic Church, and a willingness to admit persons with that status on a temporary basis to communion in the Church of England and to government in the Church of England at the parochial level.

A Roman Catholic confirmation is however recognised in Canon B28. Under that Canon

> If any ... person has been baptised but not episcopally confirmed and desires to be formally admitted into the Church of England he shall, after appropriate instruction, be received by the rite of confirmation, or if he be not yet ready to be presented for confirmation, he shall be received by the parish priest with appropriate prayers.
> If any such person has been episcopally confirmed with unction or with the laying on of hands he shall be instructed, and, with the permission of the bishop, received into the Church of England according to the Form of Reception approved by the General Synod, or with other appropriate prayers ...

Thus, Roman Catholics who have been confirmed (provided this was by the bishop, as is the norm) do not have to be confirmed again as part of their admission into the Church of England. The canonical position is unclear where Roman Catholics have been confirmed by a priest[249].

---

[249] Christian Initiation - A Policy for the Church of England says at page 42 that "we normally confirm members of non-episcopal churches, but accept without confirmation confirmed members of, for example, the Roman Catholic Church, even though they may have been confirmed by a priest". If this is correct, this is uncanonical.
The rite involves the postulant placing his hands into the hands of the priest, and the priest saying: "I, ..., acting under the Authority of our Father in God,

Chapter Eleven

Ecumenical confirmation celebrations

Canon B43 paragraph 2 (b) (iii) allows a bishop, under stated conditions, to participate in the Confirmation service of another Church. In particular, the bishop must obtain the approval

a) of the incumbent of the parish in which the service is to take place,
b) if the service takes place in another diocese, of the bishop of that diocese, and
c) of the archbishop of the province

Under Canon B44 paragraph 4 (1) (e)

A bishop who has given his agreement to participation in a local ecumenical project under the foregoing provisions of this Canon may by an instrument in writing made after consultation with the parochial church council of the project

...

(e) make provision for the holding in that area of joint services with any other participating Church, including services of baptism and confirmation.

..., Bishop of ..., receive you ... into the Church of England: in the name of the Father and of the Son and of the Holy Spirit. Amen." See the diocesan regulations for Bath and Wells, where it is emphasised that the reception may be done by a priest, rather than by the bishop. The regulations for Liverpool go further: "[Receiving from the Roman Catholic Church] should never be done by the Bishop". See also the diocesan regulations for Norwich and Lichfield.

Smethurst: Acts of Convocation at pages 165 - 169 sets out the form of reception, as adopted by the two Houses of Canterbury in 1952. See also Riley and Graham at pages 112 - 115. The rubric to the form states that the bishop may himself admit the postulant, or he may depute a priest in his stead to use the form.

The Ecumenical Relations, Canons B43 and B44: Code of Practice sets out guidelines on joint confirmations in local ecumenical projects. For example, the point is made that for the Church of England the minister of Confirmation

> must be the bishop of the diocese or some other bishop authorised by him. For some other churches it is the local minister or another minister representing the wider church. As Joint Confirmations are seen as admitting people to fellowship with the other participating Churches it is confusing, and therefore undesirable, for a local Church of England priest whose ministry is officially recognised by another Church to be that Church's officiating minister of confirmation; such a practice would in any case be contrary to Canon B43 paragraph 3(a).

The Ecumenical Relations, Canons B43 and B44: Code of Practice says that sections 23-26 of the Alternative Service Book Baptism and Confirmation Service have normally been used in joint services of confirmation, and recommends

> It is probably wise to continue this practice although a bishop might use other rites if he were satisfied that they were compatible with Church of England doctrine and practice.

Chapter Twelve

Summary and Conclusions

The following conclusions can be drawn from this study.

The theology of confirmation

Every time a congregation declares its belief at the Eucharist in the words of the Nicene Creed it is important to realise that what was denoted by the framers of the phrase "one Baptism for the remission of sins" included not only the washing with water in the name of the Trinity but also the "sealing" of this by the bishop in confirmation[250].

Seen as a sacrament of initiation, with the standard rite being the adult rite incorporating both baptism and confirmation, the theologies of the Roman Catholic church and the Church of England have much in common. The two Churches are furthest apart where the Church of England sees confirmation as merely declaratory, or an adult rite symbolising in the main the commitment of the candidate, rather than the grace of God[251].

Both churches have other services at which the promises made at baptism can be affirmed by the whole congregation, and more use should be made of these services so that the historic understanding of confirmation can be restored.

---

[250] The Welsh for "confirmation" – Bedydd Esgob (literally, *bishop's baptism*) – is a reminder of this historical fact. See Essays in Canon Law, A study of the law of the Church in Wales, at page 129.

[251] *cf.* On the Way paragraph 3.42: "Reliance on grace is the mainspring of Christian living and must not be undermined by the process of initiation".

The legal effects of confirmation

Both Churches make confirmation a condition for ordination. The Church of England makes confirmation a condition for most lay offices, and it is arguable that the same applies in the Roman Catholic Church.

The Church of England differs from the Church of Rome in allowing Communion in the main only to those who are confirmed, or who are ready and desirous of being confirmed. But there has been much debate recently on the issue whether children should be permitted to take communion before being confirmed. The survey of diocesan practice shows that several dioceses are permitting this to take place on an experimental basis, and the report of the Culham College Institute[252] shows the success of these experiments.

The proof and record of confirmation

Both Churches provide for confirmations to be recorded in a register, and for both Churches in England and Wales, confirmation registers are kept for each parish. Both Churches provide certificates of confirmation to candidates when they have been confirmed.

The age for confirmation

A cursory look at the rules would suggest that Roman Catholic children are confirmed at the age of about seven, and Church of England children at the age of about 12. However an examination of diocesan practice reveals a different picture. In many countries Roman Catholic children are confirmed at the age of 11 or 12, and in many Church of England dioceses in England, bishops are willing to confirm children from the age of nine or ten, and some as early as seven or eight, provided they are satisfied that the children will have the support to continue to grow as Christians thereafter. One cannot push this as far as to say that the diocesan practice is almost the reverse of what the rules suggest. But clearly, there is great flexibility on the issue.

---

[252] Communion before Confirmation

In many countries the Roman Catholic Church admits children to communion before confirmation, and many dioceses in the Church of England permit this to take place in some parishes. Clearly, the lower the general age for confirmation of children, the less the need to amend the canon law restricting communion to those who have been confirmed or who are ready and desirous to be confirmed.

It is the thesis of the author that confirmation should be administered at a much younger age than has traditionally been the practice in this country. As a corollary, more use should be made of the opportunity for adults to reaffirm their faith publicly in the forms of service for the renewal of baptismal promises[253].

Preparation for confirmation

In both Churches there is a tension between the Church wishing to take the opportunity to instruct the candidates for confirmation as much as possible, and the theological and liturgical desire for confirmation not to be postponed too long after baptism. The rules for both Churches emphasise the importance of preparation for confirmation: but the more the emphasis is placed on preparation, the less confirmation is seen as a sacrament of grace. I quote from a sermon delivered by the Bishop of Norwich on Maundy Thursday 1994:

> I would encourage younger children than teenagers to be presented for confirmation. Of course their understanding is limited, but is the devotion of a young boy or girl receiving the sacrament of communion less acceptable to God than that of the mature adult? Quite young children are capable of appreciating the mystery and wonder of God's grace instinctively, inarticulately. Confirmation is a means of grace not a school for commitment. I believe we need to recover the primacy of grace in Baptism and Confirmation, and to accept

---

[253] *cf.* On the Way paragraphs 5.46 and 6.9.

that commitment comes second, and is not a condition for receiving grace.[254]

Look again at the picture by Nicholas Poussin (1594-1665) reproduced at the front of this study; and may both the Roman Catholic church and the Church of England once again confirm children this young.

Who administers confirmation?

In the Roman Catholic church, the ordinary minister is a bishop, but in some cases an ordinary priest may confirm (see *e.g.* the Poussin picture). In the Church of England, only the bishop may confirm. The Church of England should consider whether this should remain the position.

After-care

The Roman Catholic rules provide for sponsors, whose functions include taking care that the person confirmed behaves as a true witness of Christ and faithfully fulfils the duties inherent in the sacrament. The Rite of Christian Initiation of Adults stresses the importance of after-care, and describes the "post-baptismal catechesis" as a time for deepening the Christian experience, for spiritual growth, and for entering more fully into the life and unity of the community[255].

At first sight the Church of England rules do not provide for after-care at all. It is only when one examines the rules at the diocesan level, and ascertains diocesan practice over the confirmation of young children, that one sees provision for after-care.

Clearly, after-care should be encouraged, and not just for children. For this to become the norm, Canon law should be altered at the national level, so that godparents others close to the candidate, and the local

---

[254] I am indebted to the Bishop of Norwich for providing me with a copy of his sermon.

[255] The Rite of Christian Initiation of Adults paragraph 7.

congregation should understand that their role includes helping the candidate to grow into Christian maturity after confirmation[256].

Change of name at confirmation

The practice of changing a person's Christian name at confirmation is an anomaly, but with a pedigree in the Church of England dating back to the reign of Elizabeth 1st, if not earlier, and also in use in the Roman Catholic Church. It is comparatively well known[257], and there seems no good reason to abolish it.

Confirmation and church membership

For the Roman Catholic the duties of church membership begin with baptism, and are carefully set out in the Code. For the Church of England, there is no clear definition of church membership, though it is established that a person who is baptised and confirmed into the Church of England, and who is a regular communicant, is a member. There is very little in the canons on the duties of church members, but there is a very helpful summary of the duties of church membership for persons who have been baptised and confirmed being that issued by the archbishops of Canterbury and York in 1954[258]. More publicity should be given to this summary, or to the earlier and fuller statement of October, 1953, by embodying one or other version in the Canons.

Confirmation in ecumenical relations

Both Churches express their desire to co-operate in the ecumenical movement, but there is great difficulty in applying this in the case of the

---

[256] see On the Way paragraph 8.4 as to the implication for local parishes.

[257] It is referred to in Halsbury's Laws of England, 4th Ed., Vol. 14 paragraph 1,000, and in Halsbury's Laws of England, 4th Ed., Vol. 35 paragraph 1273

[258] reprinted in John Stott: Your Confirmation, Hodder and Stoughton 1958 page 117.

sacraments. For example, whilst the Canons of the Church of England permit Roman Catholics to take Holy Communion in the Church of England on a temporary basis, the Canons of the Roman Catholic Church do not permit Roman Catholics to avail themselves of this privilege, save in exceptional circumstances. Nor do the Canons of the Roman Catholic Church permit their ministers to administer Holy Communion to non-Roman Catholics, save in exceptional circumstances.

The Roman Catholic Church does not recognise the validity of a Church of England confirmation, so a person who has been confirmed in the Church of England is confirmed (or re-confirmed) as part of his reception into the Roman Catholic Church. Likewise the Church of England recognises the validity of a Roman Catholic confirmation, provided this was carried out by a bishop, and possibly even if it was carried out only by a priest. Reception into the Church of England is normally by the rite of Confirmation. But if the person wishing to be received into the Church of England has already been confirmed by a bishop, the rite of confirmation is not repeated.

There needs to be clarification of the status of a Roman Catholic who is received into the Church of England without confirmation: this should be made canonically equivalent to confirmation[259]. A fortiori, a Roman Catholic who was confirmed by a priest before being received into the Church of England should be treated canonically as though validly confirmed. On the Way[260] refers to the Porvoo Declaration, and the suggestion by the Bishop of Grimsby that

> the Church of England may be willing to consider legislation to provide that references to confirmation should be interpreted as meaning either confirmation by a bishop or confirmation by a priest in an episcopally ordered Church in communion with the Church of England.

I see no reason why such legislation should be limited to the churches which are parties to the Porvoo Declaration[261].

---

[259] *cf.* On the Way paragraph 4.54.

[260] at paragraph 4.57.

[261] see also On the Way paragraph 7.14

The Church of England has legislation for joint confirmation services with other denominations, and both legislation and guidance notes for use where this forms part of a local ecumenical project. The requirement under Canon B43 that the consent of an archbishop be obtained for a joint confirmation service indicates that the Church of England is moving in this direction only very cautiously. The Roman Catholic Church is even more cautious in not permitting joint confirmation services at all.

The last word

Confirmation has historically always been an important part of a Christian's initiation. Indeed, to quote St. Thomas Aquinas

> Hoc enim sacramentum est perfectio baptismi. ... Sic igitur vitam spiritualem homo accipit per baptismum, qui est spiritualis regeneratio. In confirmatione autem home accipit quasi quandam aetatem perfectam spiritualis vitae[262].

---

[262] *i.e.* "The sacrament is the completion of baptism....In this way, therefore, man receives [the] spiritual life through baptism, which is the rebirth of the spirit. However when he is confirmed, man accepts that a certain stage of his spiritual life has been completed". St Thomas Aquinas: *Summa Theologica* 3, 72, 1. The Latin text is quoted in Lampe: The Seal of the Spirit, at page 309. J.D.C. Fisher: Christian Initiation: Baptism in the Medieval West, page 129, translates the passage as follows: "So also, man receives spiritual life through baptism, which is spiritual regeneration: but in confirmation man receives a kind of perfect age of the spiritual life".

But confirmation is not the end of the road. In St. Paul's command to the Ephesian Church "be filled with the Spirit"[263], the context, and the tense of the Greek word πληροῦσθε[264], show that the command "be filled" is a continuing obligation. Christians must go on being filled with the Spirit, and depending on the grace of God.

---

[263] Ephesians 5:18.
[264] *i.e. pleeroústhe*, the present, rather than the aorist, imperative.

APPENDIX

The Code of Canon Law

Book IV. The Sanctifying Office of the Church.

Title II. The Sacrament of Confirmation

Chapter I The Celebration of Confirmation

Canon 879

The sacrament of confirmation confers a character. By it the baptised continue their path of Christian initiation. They are enriched with the gift of the Holy Spirit, and are more closely linked to the Church. They are made strong and more firmly obliged by word and deed to witness to Christ and to spread and defend the faith.

Canon 880

§ 1. The sacrament of confirmation is conferred by anointing with chrism on the forehead, which is done by the laying on of the hand, and by the words prescribed in the approved liturgical books.
§ 2. The chrism to be used in the sacrament of confirmation must have been consecrated by a Bishop, even when the sacrament is administered by a priest.

Canon 881

It is desirable that the sacrament of confirmation be celebrated in a church and indeed during Mass. However, for a just and reasonable cause it may be celebrated apart from Mass and in any fitting place.

Chapter II The Minister of Confirmation

Canon 882

The ordinary minister of confirmation is a Bishop. A priest can also validly confer this sacrament if he has the faculty to do so, either from the universal law or by way of a special grant from the competent authority.

Canon 883

The following have, by law, the faculty to administer confirmation:
1. within the confines of their jurisdiction, those who in law are equivalent to a diocesan Bishop;
2. in respect of the person to be confirmed, the priest who by virtue of his office or by mandate of the diocesan Bishop baptises one who is no longer an infant or admits a person already baptised into full communion with the catholic Church;
3. in respect of those in danger of death, the parish priest or indeed any priest.

Canon 884

§1. The diocesan Bishop is himself to administer confirmation or to ensure that it is administered by another Bishop. If necessity so requires, he may grant to one of several specified priests the faculty to administer this sacrament.
§2. For a grave reason the Bishop, or the priest who by law of by special grant of the competent authority has the faculty to confirm, may in individual cases invite other priests to join with him in administering the sacrament.

Canon 885

§1. The diocesan Bishop is bound to ensure that the sacrament of confirmation is conferred upon his subjects who duly and reasonably request it.
§2. A priest who has this faculty must use it for those in whose favour it was granted.

Canon 886

§1. A Bishop in his own diocese may lawfully administer the sacrament of confirmation even to the faithful who are not his subjects, unless there is an express prohibition by their own Ordinary.
§2. In order lawfully to administer confirmation in another diocese, unless it be to his own subjects, a Bishop needs the permission, at least reasonably presumed, of the diocesan Bishop.

Canon 887

A priest who has the faculty to administer confirmation may, within the territory assigned to him, lawfully administer the sacrament even to those from outside the territory, unless there is a prohibition by their own Ordinary. He cannot, however, validly confirm anyone in another territory, without prejudice to the provision of Canon 883 n. 3.

Canon 888

Within the territory in which they can confer confirmation, ministers may confirm even in exempt places.

Chapter III The Persons to Be Confirmed

Canon 889

§1. Every baptised person who is not confirmed, and only such a person, is capable of receiving confirmation.
§2. Apart from the danger of death, to receive confirmation lawfully a person who has the use of reason must be suitably instructed, properly disposed and able to renew the baptismal promises.

Canon 890

The faithful are bound to receive this sacrament at the proper time. Parents and pastors of souls, especially parish priests, are to see that the faithful are properly instructed to receive the sacrament and come to it at the opportune time.

Canon 891

The sacrament of confirmation is to be conferred on the faithful at about the age of discretion, unless the Bishops' Conference has decided on a different age, or there is a danger of death or, in the judgment of the minister, a grave reason suggests otherwise.

Chapter IV Sponsors

Canon 892

As far as possible the person to be confirmed is to have a sponsor. The sponsor's function is to take care that the person confirmed behaves as a true witness of Christ and faithfully fulfils the duties inherent in the sacrament.

Canon 893

§1. A person who would undertake the office of sponsor must fulfil the conditions mentioned in Canon 874.
§2. It is desirable that the sponsor chosen be the one who undertook this role at baptism.

Chapter V Proof and Registration of Confirmation

Canon 894

To establish that confirmation has been conferred, the provisions of Canon 876 are to be observed.

Canon 895

The names of those confirmed, the minister, the parents, the sponsors and the place and date of the confirmation are to be recorded in the confirmation register of the diocesan curia or, wherever this has been prescribed by the Bishops' Conference or by the diocesan Bishop, in the register to be kept in the parochial archive. The parish priest must notify the parish priest of the place of the baptism that the confirmation was conferred, so that it be recorded in the baptismal register, in accordance with Canon 535 §2.

Canon 896

If the parish priest of the place was not present, the minister, personally or through someone else, is to notify him as soon as possible that the confirmation was conferred.

The Canons of the Church of England

Section B: Divine Service and the administration of the sacraments

Canon B27 Of Confirmation

1. The bishop of every diocese shall himself minister (or cause to be ministered by some other bishop lawfully deputed in his stead) the rite of confirmation throughout his diocese as often and in as many places as shall be convenient, laying his hands upon children and other persons who have been baptised and instructed in the Christian faith.

2. Every minister who has a cure of souls shall diligently seek out children and other persons whom he shall think meet to be confirmed and shall use his best endeavour to instruct them in the Christian faith and life as set forth in the holy Scriptures, the Book of Common Prayer, and the Church Catechism.

3. The minister shall present none to the bishop but such as are come to years of discretion and can say the Creed, the Lord's Prayer, and the Ten Commandments, and can also render an account of their faith according to the said Catechism.

4. The minister shall satisfy himself that those whom he is to present have been validly baptised, ascertaining the date and place of such baptism, and, before or at the time assigned for the confirmation, shall give to the bishop their names, together with their age and the date of their baptism.

5. If the minister is doubtful about the baptism of a candidate for confirmation he shall conditionally baptise him in accordance with the

form of service authorised by Canon B 1 before presenting him to the bishop to be confirmed.

6. If it is desired for sufficient reason that a Christian name be changed, the bishop may, under the laws of this realm, confirm a person by a new Christian name, which shall be thereafter deemed the lawful Christian name of such person.

Index

actual communicant
   definition, 28
after-care, 42, 43, 44, 45, 63, 65,
   67, 98
Alpha course, 57, 98
America, 35, 51
anointing, 1, 12, 64, 87, 89
apostles, 10, 18, 19
apostolic, 76, 80
Aquinas, St Thomas, 101
archbishop, 27, 44, 92, 101
Arundel, 35
ascension, 16
Australia, 35
baptism
   acceptance of candidate for, 61
   addition of name at
      Confirmation, 70
   administered by bishop, 1
   adult, 51, 55
   adult preparation for, 51
   adult rite, 95
   baptismal name and Christian
      name, 71
   baptismal register, 72
   bishop's duty to confirm
      baptised adult, 30
   certificate of, 31
   Christian name given at, 69, 71
   church membership, 99
   Church of England sacrament,
      14
   confirmation a complement to,
      20

   confirmation delayed after, 36,
      97
   confirmation the completion of,
      101
   description of early rite, 1
   duty of mission, 77
   duty to inform bishop in case of
      adults, 29
   Eastern pattern, 38
   ecumenical recognition of, 88
   entry into Church by, 12
   formal membership of Church
      of England, 79
   gift bestowed at, 16
   grace in, 97
   in Scripture, 11
   included laying on of hands, 1
   incorporated into the Church,
      75
   incorporation into Christ, 75
   infant baptism, 1, 10, 37
   joint ecumenical services of, 92,
      93
   made God's children in
      Baptism, 18
   membership of the Church, 75
   must precede confirmation, 33
   necessary for PCC members, 28
   necessary to receive Eucharist,
      23
   necessity for burial, 29
   new birth in baptism, 18
   one Baptism for the remission
      of sins, 95
   ordained by Christ, 14